"'Data-driven' is the new competitive DNA—no one is a better student and teacher of our times and digital business than Ray Wang. This book succeeds beyond a 'how-to' in creating a belief system and urgency for change to succeed in the era of digital networks."

—Ganesh Bell, Board Advisor, Investor,
Former CDO, and Software Business CEO

"Ray Wang's take on digital duopolies caused by the rise of data oligarchs offers insights and bold strategies for all corporations for the future."

—Alan Boehme, CTO, H&M, and Former
CTO at P&G and Coca-Cola

"CEOs around the world stay connected to Ray Wang for a reason. He has the ability to accurately analyze trends and predict the future. In this book, he describes the accelerating gap between winners and losers, and we all know people are going to be a critical part of that. You should read this book and redesign your people strategy based on it."

—Michael Bush, CEO, Great Place to Work

"A must-read for CEOs, CMOs, corporate strategists, public policy makers, and investors, irrespective of industry sector. Ray Wang clearly outlines the implications of the formation of digital duopolies on corporate survival, business models, and public policy."

—Anil Cheriyan, Executive VP for
Strategy and Technology, Cognizant

"In *Everybody Wants to Rule the World*, Ray Wang delivers both a playbook for building the next digital giants and, more importantly, inspiration for leaders to build guardrails that balance free markets, innovation, open access, and equal opportunity in the world ahead."

—Aneesh Chopra, Former US CTO (2009–12)
and Cofounder and President, CareJourney

"The industry landscape in the digital era is changing, and the changes are eternal, tectonic in nature. Ray Wang deftly captures one such profound change in his new book, *Everybody Wants to Rule the World*. The rise of digital duopolies is powered by data, network effects, exponential tech, access to huge capital pools, and a winner-take-all ambition. Ray provides riveting, 360-degree insight into this exponential world and shares practical guidance on how incumbents can either become digital giants or partner with them as part of an ecosystem. To build, partner, or die. Another masterpiece from one of the top digital thinkers in the world. A must-read."

—Neetan Chopra, CTO, Dubai Holdings

"The pandemic has accelerated consolidation across industries and the digitalization of business, forcing us all to take a close look at our playbooks. Ray Wang shares a unique look into where the digital giants are headed and how to move forward as a smart, data-driven business. The digital future that Ray paints is closer than ever. I highly recommend his book to business leaders."

—Duke Chung, Cofounder and CEO, TravelBank

"With his signature style of directness, compelling evidence, and conviction, Ray Wang lays out a reality, warning, and response for business and government leaders to embrace in addressing the growing influence and implications of data-driven digital networks and the emerging digital duopolies that exploit them. Alarming on the one hand, instructive and constructive on the other. The kind of timely and important narrative we must have."

—Lanny Cohen, Executive Advisor
and Former Group CIO, Capgemini

"If you think your company has a reasonably good digital transformation agenda, this book will scare you. It paints the next chapter on digital in an ominous way, pointing to that thing that you are most worried about: your organization's decisionmaking speed and leadership. It also paints the future in a way that helps you explain it better than traditional consulting reports. I was highly inspired."

—Sandeep Dadlani, Global CDO, Mars

"A new world order of technology-centric company dominance is here. Ray Wang has developed a compelling roadmap for how leaders should invest to thrive in a new era of data- and network-driven business. All of the rules have changed; either learn them or perish."

—Crawford Del Prete,
President, International Data Corporation

"It's not about digital transformation anymore. It's about building data value chains. *Everybody Wants to Rule the World* offers several takeaways on how to get there."

—Larry Dignan, Editor-in-Chief, ZDNet,
and Editorial Director, TechRepublic

"While everyone is still talking about digital transformation, Ray Wang has unlocked how the digital giants are going after massive monetization across industries and value chains. Leaders must understand this new landscape and prepare for a shift in strategy. *Everybody Wants to Rule The World* is a must-read book that lays out the steps and business models required for success."

—Lara Druyan, Managing Director,
Silicon Valley Data Capital

"You are just getting your head around digital transformation, and you think you can't compete with digital giants. You can, and Ray Wang lays it out for you. This book gives you leapfrog powers to go from amateur fan to power player by understanding roles and opportunities in this new economy."

—Jana Eggers, CEO, Nara Logics

"This book should be on the shelf, or ideally the desk, of every Fortune 2000 executive. It highlights both what's around the corner as well as strategies to survive and thrive. Ray thoughtfully discusses 3D—digital, data, and DNA—to provide a roadmap for industry leaders. I wish he had written it a decade ago to help shape my investment thesis!"

—Mark Fernandes, Managing Partner, Sierra Ventures

"This is a rare book that can rightly claim to be both visionary and evidence-based. Ray Wang has threaded the needle in giving us this invaluable preview of the business models that will dominate the coming decades."

—John Kao, Author of *Jamming: The Art and Discipline of Business Creativity*

"Ray Wang paints a compelling picture of digital giants shaping industries, capital markets, and society at large, and charts a path for the next wave of business leaders to harness data for better, faster decisionmaking."

—Ariel Kelman, Executive VP and CMO, Oracle

"Digital transformation and networked business models are becoming imperatives for companies of all sizes and across every industry. Ray Wang's book provides a great guide to how to compete in a digital world and thrive in today's volatile environment."

—Christian Klein, CEO, SAP

"Wow! Ray Wang's vision of the future will force every industry and enterprise to examine its core purpose and beliefs. Building the future will require that these ideas be executed in an agile, iterative innovation process, at great speed."

—Ananth Krishnan, Executive VP and CTO, Tata Consultancy Services

"In his new book, *Everybody Wants to Rule the World*, Ray Wang analyses how the tidal forces of change at the core of the fourth industrial revolution are reshaping our societies and forever changing the way we live. A must-read."

—Frederic Laluyaux, President and CEO, Aera Technology

"Powerful and insightful: this book will teach you how to turn down the noise and tune into the market signals that matter most. A must-read for every leader tasked with designing and delivering the future of customer connection and value creation."

—Karen Mangia, Author of *Working from Home*, *Listen Up!*, and *Success With Less*

"Ray Wang's book is fantastic. It does a great job of projecting the likely consequences of the rise of data-driven businesses that leverage massive scale and network effects in every industry, offering us advice on how to thrive in this environment. A must-read for entrepreneurs, Fortune 500 executives, regulators, and everyone else who wants to get ready!"

—Alexander Rinke, CEO, Celonis

"Digital transformation is not a luxury anymore but a necessity. And it is hardly only about technology. The biggest challenge is to engage and drive tangible business results through digital platforms, which requires slowly changing the DNA of your organization. Ray Wang is a strategic global thinker, and in this book he depicts the topics that every organization should understand and leverage to stay ahead of the curve. It is the time to disrupt or be disrupted. Well done, Ray!"

—Sanjib Sahoo, Award-winning CIO,
CDO, and BT150 Winner for 2020

"Ray Wang is one of the best-connected people I know. His conferences include executives from multiple industries, and this gives him insights into business shifts few see. Here you will learn about a huge shift underway that is disrupting industries from transportation to healthcare. Will yours be next? You better read this to find out."

—Robert Scoble, Futurist

"Leaders who seek a path forward in today's winner-takes-all economy must read Ray Wang's book to understand how to navigate and counter the macro forces in play and understand their impact on commerce, politics, and society."

—Clara Shih, CEO, Salesforce Service Cloud
and Hearsay Social, and Author of *The Facebook Era*

"Digital giants were first to understand and take advantage of signal intelligence. Ray Wang's book, *Everybody Wants to Rule the World,* contains vital insights and warnings for businesses looking to survive and thrive in an ever-expanding digital world."

—John Sicard, CEO, Kinaxis

"To a business and technology leader, the business model shifts have never been so apparent. However, Ray Wang's insights into new monetization models and the battle for data supremacy are a rude awakening that every leader should design for in their future plans."

—Rhonda Vetere, Executive VP and Global CIO, Herbalife Nutrition, Author, and Triathlete

"In *Everybody Wants to Rule the World,* Ray Wang reveals the digital giants' DNA and divulges where they are going next—showing the next generation of leaders what it takes to keep up and leap ahead."

—Maynard Webb, Founder, Webb Investment Network, and Former COO, eBay and Webb Investment

"Dancing with 800-pound digital gorillas requires agility, skill, and the world's best dance instructor, Ray Wang. Read this book to waltz your way into creating competitive advantage in the new economy."

—Soon Yu, Bestselling Author of *Iconic Advantage*

"Rarely does a book on the digital future present the big picture while also sweating the details that make up the digital canvas that is disrupting and delivering our futures. Filled with insight, stories, and examples, this book is a must-read to help business leaders and their teams bring their digital futures into focus."

—Bob Zukis, CEO, Digital Directors Network, and USC Marshall Professor

R "RAY" WANG

EVERYBODY
WANTS TO
RULE THE
WORLD

SURVIVING AND THRIVING
IN A WORLD OF DIGITAL GIANTS

HarperCollins
LEADERSHIP

An imprint of HarperCollins

*To my parents for their never-ending belief in their kids
and the unlimited possibilities of the American Dream,
and to my family for the countless amounts of shared sacrifice
in putting up with my crazy pursuits.*

Published by HarperCollins Leadership, an imprint of HarperCollins Focus LLC.

Any internet addresses, phone numbers, or company or product information printed in this book are offered as a resource and are not intended in any way to be or to imply an endorsement by HarperCollins Leadership, nor does HarperCollins Leadership vouch for the existence, content, or services of these sites, phone numbers, companies, or products beyond the life of this book.

ISBN 978-1-4002-2473-9 (eBook)

ISBN 978-1-4002-2486-9 (HC)

Library of Congress Control Number: 2021937290

Printed in the United States of America

21 22 23 24 25 LSC 10 9 8 7 6 5 4 3 2 1

CONTENTS

INTRODUCTION

What you are about to read comes from the synthesis and analysis of over ten thousand conversations, design sessions, and strategy meetings with some of the top digital transformation clients, partners, gurus, academics, and thought leaders since 2015. The launch of my first book, *Disrupting Digital Business*, put digital transformation on the map for many. The realization that digital technologies, along with new digital business models, would create a massive disruption was still a bit early for the market. Yet, since 2010, my firm, Constellation Research, has attracted a community of over a thousand executives, vendor partners, and academics who are leading the digital transformation charge.

These individuals and the companies and organizations they represent are the leaders in their field. Their ability to drive business model transformation, apply the exponential technologies, and lead cultural change puts them in a league of their own. In fact, these folks, whom we call "change agents," represent the top global executives leading business transformation efforts in their organizations. Since 2010, we have identified the top 150 for their contributions to digital and business transformation. Since 2016, we have published and recognized a definitive list of business transformation leaders, the BT150, every year at our annual executive innovation summit, Constellation Connected Enterprise.

Sometime in 2018, our conversations with this elite group of experts turned to an analysis of why digital transformation efforts had succeeded or failed. The post-mortem analysis of the programs they led identified a factor that had not been considered—the playing field had changed. For many industries, the field had massively changed. Direct head-on competition no longer seemed to be the game. A rash of mergers and acquisitions took a vertically integrated stance that was more aligned with value chains than industries. Nontraditional competitors entered the market seemingly from thin air. These new entrants were well-funded and could absorb massive losses to gain market share. Moreover, these organizations envisioned a new market that had not existed before. They were entering the market from a position that at first seemed untenable but then became massively viral, overnight.

At the same time, companies that had built digital monetization models started to gain traction with customers and the investment community. While technology companies pioneered and perfected the *software as a service* model (SaaS), or what we now call cloud computing, other industries were also building out new monetization models for digital business. These organizations were across all industries—in advertising, digital goods, digital services, memberships, search, and subscriptions.

In 2006, I remembered hearing from Tien Tzuo, a brilliant entrepreneur and friend, who at the time was the CMO of Salesforce.com, an emerging customer relationship management software company. He was talking about the end of ownership, the push to subscription revenues. New companies had to have new subscription models in order to be the winners in the market. He ended up leaving Salesforce.com to found Zuora, a company which evangelized the subscription economy. He was probably ahead of the market by five years, but he was onto something big. New digital monetization models were at the heart of a revolution as Wall Street began to embrace recurring revenue. They liked the predictability and they loved the IPOs to come. He was right and truly a visionary.

Meanwhile, large tech companies and tech-related firms gained ground in the daily lives of humanity. Soon every part of society had a tech component, from dating to food delivery to healthcare to spiritual advice. The rise of search, social media giants, ride-hailing services, online commerce, digital advertising, the app economy, and dating put big tech on the map for creating jobs, inspiring innovation, and changing the world. Tech-related companies were disrupting traditional industries. Soon startups were popping up that challenged every industry, including financial (FinTech), healthcare (HealthTech), government and public sector (GovTech), and online commerce. Sadly there wasn't a category call for RetailTech. No sector was untouched.

But the world came to a screeching halt almost right after Davos in January 2020. The fallout from COVID-19 hit the global economy hard. Just months prior, almost every economist had forecast a great year, and an awesome year in the United States. Businesses were gearing up massive investments to support 2020. Companies had planned to invest more in digital technologies, automation, cloud computing, and artificial intelligence. Every organization had begun an effort to improve their talent management and recruiting as there were not enough employees to fill all the job openings. Travel, retail, hospitality, entertainment, and professional sports were upping their investments in loyalty, customer experience, and amenities to attract more customers.

When the virus hit the US in March 2020, all pre-pandemic plans were thrown out the window. The restriction on movement put an end to density as a business model. Those entities that could shift fast or had exiting digital business models grew stronger as their competitors went bankrupt. Billions of people lost their jobs, especially those who did not have jobs that could work from home.

The growing correlation between digital businesses and winner-take-all markets became clearer to a few folks studying the shifts in the market. Anand Giridharadas's 2018 book, aptly titled *Winners Take All*, showed how the elites had rigged the system under the guise of public good or social change. His analysis on the devastating impact of how many forces in philanthrocapitalism had worked together to rig markets and exacerbate the social divide was coming true. In addition, the 2017 work of Scott Galloway, *The Four*, highlighted how the tech giants Amazon, Apple, Facebook, and Google had infiltrated our lives so completely that they're almost impossible to avoid. These companies were clearly the post-pandemic winners.

Somewhere along the way I gained clarity on who would emerge as the winners and losers in the market. At first it was hard to pinpoint the factors. Digital was a component but not the only attribute that mattered. Data was the foundation of digital businesses, but I wondered what type of data was most important. I postulated that easy access to capital was part of the shift, but quickly realized the good ideas had no issue with funding. I examined what was required in terms of technology and realized that artificial intelligence (AI) would play a huge role forward. I started to build models and write big idea papers from 2016 to 2020 that had pieces of the puzzle. Many of you who read those wondered how it would all come together. I did too!

It finally all made sense to me one day when I was sitting in my house cleaning up the basement. We had built a new home four years earlier, and like all good basements, the collection of all things forgotten was conveniently sheltered in one place. I had thirty-five crates of vinyl records, lots of old electronics equipment, laser discs, CDs, DVDs, mix tapes, turntables, analog lighting. As I was rummaging through my life and trying to put it in some order, I realized that we were in the midst of a transition. With my last box of goods I no longer needed donated to the local charity, I discovered that the reason I had so much junk in the basement was because the world had truly gone digital.

All those items in my house no longer were needed because they had been replaced by software or a digital service. (I did keep the 10,000 watt speakers, turntables, and vinyl for nostalgia purposes and for when I do DJ a set.) I had dived right into a digital world without even realizing it. I had changed my business models. I had become a subscriber to music. I had a membership to DJ software. I had willingly shared data on my likes and preferences in exchange for better personalization. I was powering the future digital giants in content, distribution, monetization, and experience.

Everybody Wants to Rule the World was written to help leaders not only understand this shift and build worthy competitors but also craft the guiderails required to keep the digital giants in check and enable innovation in fair and free markets. The rise of these digital giants requires a different mindset for success and regulation. It's true that between March 2020 and August 2020, what would have taken five years to accelerate to digital occurred in five months of COVID-19. However, while that may have sped up digital transformation, it did nothing to halt the rise of the digital giants.

Understanding the digital giants' DNA, how they operate, why they continue to build exponential barriers to entry, and where their next foray will take them will help the next generation of leaders prepare for an environment where "everybody wants to rule the world." The first chapters tell you how to build a digital giant. The middle chapters provide guidelines for policymakers ensuring we have free market competition and a proper amount of regulations to balance innovation with antitrust. The last chapters of the book show you how to partner to compete and describe how the digital giants will evolve.

I'm really looking forward to your reactions and feedback. The field is emerging, but the trends move fast. So, don't hesitate to reach out to me by email or through Twitter—or just pull me aside and say hello. There's so much going on and so much to share. Whether your role is building, partnering, or even regulating the digital giants, I look forward to the conversation ahead.

Enjoy!

EVERYBODY WANTS
TO RULE THE WORLD

1

THE RISE OF DUOPOLIES

*"Either be number one or number two in your industry or get out!
Companies win by getting bigger and ultimately dominating industries."*
—JACK WELCH[1]

The most popular business buzz-phrase of the 2010s was "digital transformation." The technology trend that began in the 1990s when the World Wide Web first came into our lives and started changing how we do business was spreading at a feverish pace throughout the entire Fortune 500 as cloud computing, mobile technologies, social networks, data analytics, and AI proliferated. Companies were changing business models and processes, customer experiences, and even their company's culture using new technologies.

After surviving the financial crisis of 2008, big companies that weren't already in mid-transformation made a mad dash to become more digital, to take more market share, and to spread their reach into other sectors. Retailers such as Kroger's, Macy's, Metro Group, and Walmart invested heavily in digital commerce to support their buy-online-pick-up-in-store capabilities. Pharmacies such as CVS bought health insurers such as Aetna, vertically integrating healthcare. Comcast acquired content producers such as Universal NBC to fend off streaming competitors such as Netflix, while telecommunication giant Verizon bought AOL Yahoo to become a global media company. Large real estate investment trusts and commercial office space operators invested in the Internet of Things (IoT) to enable smart buildings and smart cities. Even Toyota made big bets outside of its core business with Woven City, a 175-acre prototype "city of the future" fueled by hydrogen fuel cells.

Meanwhile, startups with venture capital funding became more ambitious and impatient than ever. With ever-increasing valuation, startups like Uber, Airbnb, Beyond Meat, and WeWork used their stock price as currency to fuel their growth. Their CEOs began hiring aggressively, acquiring their competitors, and hoarding key resources. Their goal? To take market share and disrupt the business of organizations that had been around for far longer. That was their reason for being: They were designed from day one to dominate their markets, overthrow the Fortune 500, and emerge as monopolies. The result was an unprecedented shift in the entire business climate. Sector after sector became a winner-takes-all—or two-winners-take-all—bloodbath. Facebook dominated social media. Amazon took over commerce. Google ruled search. Netflix won the streaming wars. Add the global COVID-19 pandemic in March 2020, and the gaps between winners and losers not only widened, but the pace of change also accelerated.

Duopolies are forever changing when and how we buy, where we bank, and how our data is used. Make no mistake: Their rise represents a life-or-death challenge for your company—no matter what sector you're in or how long you've held a secure position. In *Everybody Wants to Rule the World*, I will you show you the disruption and opportunity ahead of you and your organization—and how you can embark on a path to not only survive, but also thrive in the age of digital duopolies. But before I do so, let's start by understanding exactly how we got here, so we can better prepare for the challenges ahead.

The Emergence of DDDNs and the Quest to Rule the World

The ambition to become a monopoly—to dominate a market—of course, is nothing new. In fact, consolidation has been a feature of global business since at least the railroad boom of the late nineteenth century. Most successful regional players dream of emerging as a top contender in the nation. Once they grow to play in the national stage, they set their sights toward global domination. In the highly competitive pizza delivery market, for example, Domino's, founded in Michigan in 1960, and Pizza Hut, also founded in Michigan only two years earlier, duked it out for five *decades* before they beat competitors like Little Caesars, Papa John, Sbarro, and others to emerge as national and then global duopolies. These two once-regional players entered the international stage more than ten years after they started operating, when Pizza Hut opened its first Canadian franchise in 1968 and Domino's opened its own in 1983. Since then, they've battled for markets such as India and China, with Domino's overtaking Pizza Hut in global revenue in 2018.

Countless industries went through gradual reorganization from hundreds or thousands of small regional players down to a couple of giants, like Domino's and Pizza Hut did. Think of Coke versus Pepsi in soft drinks, MasterCard versus Visa in credit cards, Boeing versus Airbus in airplane manufacturing. But until very recently, the key word was "gradual."

Today's monopolies and duopolies aren't the result of a natural, almost haphazard evolution of mature markets. Instead, they are often deliberately and ruthlessly constructed from day one, commonly as what I call data-driven digital networks (DDDN). A DDDN is any business that captures, harnesses, and deploys insights from massive amounts of data, often provided for "free" by a large network of users. The biggest examples of DDDNs are the dominant companies of our time: Google uses your search data to sell ads specifically targeted to you in exchange for free services such as its Gmail application. Amazon uses data about the purchases you've made on its site to sell you even more stuff. Facebook encourages you to build a network and share content with it so they can sell ads based on your profile and preferences.

The more quality data these DDDNs collect and analyze, the more accurately they can target users with more appealing products, services, and advertising . . . which leads to more user engagement . . . which leads to even more data collection . . . which leads to even more powerful marketing. In fact, this leaves no room for competitors because the user is caught in a closed ecosystem. This flywheel effect drives the exponential dominance of DDDNs.

Now, DDDNs apply these massive digital feedback loops to all of their stakeholders—customers, employees, suppliers, partners—and use data-driven insights to mitigate risk, identify new opportunities, improve operational efficiency, anticipate customer demands, and drive dynamic pricing. For example, Google can automatically and dynamically adjust ad pricing based on the popularity of a search term or engagement in a topic. Amazon can identify which routes and markets to expand based on logistic costs and profit margins. By relying on technologies such as AI and the cloud at scale, DDDNs automate many data-driven decisions—such as what products and services to promote in what markets and at what price. This gives them an unfair competitive advantage and makes it even harder for non-DDDNs to succeed.

The results from these network effects have been truly extraordinary. Over the past decade, DDDNs have raced to acquire millions of users, then hundreds of millions, then in some cases even billions. Facebook, founded just fifteen years ago, now has 2.5 billion registered users—about a third of the entire global population. Now that's a growth curve! The meteoric growth of DDDNs is only matched by their growth in market cap value. DDDNs such as Google, Amazon, Microsoft, and Apple are part of the Trillion Dollar Trade, a term that referenced their trillion dollar market cap values before the coronavirus (BC) pandemic. These companies also have accumulated more cash on hand than most companies, with almost half a trillion U.S. dollars among Microsoft, Google, Apple, Amazon, and Facebook.

But building a DDDN is hard. It requires a combination of massive computing power, products or services that engage users, AI, and billions in capital investment—a high barrier to entry that ensures only a few players in any market succeed in doing so. If a DDDN already has a foothold in a market, the power of its virtuous digital data feedback loop makes it harder and harder for competitors to catch up to it. Even if they are not already in a market, DDDNs can use their dominance in another market and their value chains to enter new ones much more easily. Most of their competitors are taken by surprise and fail to react on time.

But even those who try to mount a defense have found it an uphill battle, especially since their ability to do the very thing that could save them—investing in innovation—has been largely quashed by a hostile investment environment.

Irrational Investing and the Decline of Innovation

The story of how established companies got hung out to dry by investors begins in the 2010s. That decade saw the financial markets skewed by the concentration of more and more investment capital among the "mega-investor" class. My firm, Constellation Research, found that just thirty shareholders control 51.4 percent of the assets of 299 of the Fortune 500 companies. Today, institutional investors like BlackRock, Vanguard, and State Street control two-thirds of all U.S. equities. In 1970, by contrast, the same number was controlled more widely by a greater number of private individuals and families.

This mega-investor class also invested heavily in venture capital (VC) funds that backed disruptive startups such as Alibaba, Facebook, Flipkart, JD.com, Snap, and Spotify. In 2008 there were about a hundred VC funds with $28.8 billion invested in 2,550 deals. By 2017—not even a decade later—there were nearly six hundred VC funds with $82 billion invested in more than 9,000 deals. This 400 percent increase in investment funding and in the number of startups created an explosion of speculation and risk-taking. In the quest for greater and greater yield, startups that disrupted traditional businesses were high risk, yet high return bets.

As the 2008 financial crisis subsided, the C-Suites of the Fortune 500 stood in fear of those well-funded startups determined to disrupt their business models with cutting-edge technology. The old guys finally opened their checkbooks for digital transformation initiatives that they hoped would help them compete. Unfortunately for most of them, those investments were too little, too late. Macy's efforts to move to a digital strategy, for example, drained resources and cannibalized existing store revenue, leading to a decade of declining revenue growth. General Electric's failed attempt at digital transformation led to a massive decline and a staggering $500,000,000,000 in market cap loss for the venerable Dow component.[2] In many sectors, the digital divide was already starting to accelerate, with consolidation much faster than ever before—often devastatingly fast—resulting in one or two DDDNs already on their way toward monopoly or duopoly status.

To add insult to injury, the mega-investors who should have been pushing the Fortune 500 to invest more in digital transformation to compete against these DDDNs instead became more conservative, demanding higher and higher quarterly profits. For many years now, these institutional investors had been losing sleep over one of their most significant obligations: The pending retirement of baby boomers by 2030. They were counting on their established investments to deliver a consistent return.

But despite taking a conservative approach with their investments in established companies, the same investors willingly hedged big bets on startups. In fact, investors began extracting every bit of cash from these well-established portfolio companies and using that cash to make aggressive investments in disruptive startups—in the very same or adjacent markets! Somehow, investing millions in startups appeared to be less risky than properly funding traditional companies to innovate and compete against nontraditional players.

So just when large incumbent companies should have gone full out to defend against digital disruption, most of them pulled back, cutting their spending on long-term R&D. Decades of cost-cutting, mergers and acquisitions, and activist shareholder fights had already decimated the growth and innovation culture at many organizations. In a graph often cited by the late Clayton Christensen, a noted expert on disruptive innovation, in 1981, 50 percent of the average investment of profits was allocated to research and development and 50 percent to shareholder dividends. Today, 50 percent of that investment is allocated to stock buybacks, 49 percent to dividends, and a meager 1 percent to research and development.[3] Essentially, the market has been punishing incumbent companies that choose to innovate, leading to wave after wave of terrible decisions over a series of business cycles.

Many established companies compensated for their lack of organic growth—typically fueled by R&D—by turning to the dark arts of financial engineering instead. Greedy management teams colluded with short-term shareholders to waste precious capital on stock buybacks, dividends, and other ways to make a company look good on paper. If you were a Fortune 500 executive, this was a great strategy if your priority was earning a bonus tied to "shareholder value." But it was not such a great strategy if your priority was helping your company survive digital disruption. Starved of capital and focused on short-term profits, they got even weaker just when they needed to get stronger.

Meanwhile, this winner-takes-all investment approach was having a nearly opposite but equally bad impact on all those well-funded, VC-controlled startups. Under tremendous pressure to get big and dominate their sectors as fast as possible, these startups began to run huge losses to grab market share and damage the incumbents. Profit and business models went out the window as a short-term or even medium-term goal, pushed back to the distant future. Nearly every startup of the 2010s (think of We-Work, Instagram, Uber, Slack, Theranos) wanted to be like the startups of the 2000s such as Amazon: grow like crazy, establish a monopoly or duopoly, then have faith that profits would follow. If that required a business model that was basically selling a dime for a nickel, so be it. The VCs only seemed to care about top-line revenue growth. Eventually, the cracks in these startups' indefensible business models started to form, leading most of them to fail and leaving only a few unicorns with solid business models to emerge.

Extreme Monetization—the Final Nail in the Coffin

Irrational investing prevented established companies from funding the innovations they needed to compete against DDDNs in their core market. But even those companies that invested in digital transformation were still blindsided by big DDDNs from other sectors that increasingly moving into theirs. Before they even realized what happened, traditional companies were pushed out.

In the industrial age, business models and monetization models were basically the same thing. Each sector had a clear business model (such as selling more pizza, trucks, cola, or magazines) and a matching monetization model for generating revenue (such as B2B sales, B2C sales, subscriptions, or advertising). The lanes between sectors were clearly defined. *Time* competed with *Newsweek* for national print ads, while Coke competed with Pepsi for supermarket shelf space and vending machine sales. Domino's competed with Pizza Hut for best pizza franchise experience.

But in the digital age, two companies can have the same business model—the same way to design, create, capture, and deliver value—but very different ways to monetize that value. For example, LinkedIn and Twitter have different business models. LinkedIn is focused on being the resume of record for a business professional community and Twitter is a social media platform. Yet, they both are in the business of selling ads. This fluidity has scrambled the traditional lanes between sectors, allowing a company like Amazon to expand the Prime monetization model (an annual subscription) from retail to many other sectors, including TV and movie production. When you are a DDDN, you have the network power to try to spread across as many lanes as you like, swallowing new competitors and dominating even more sectors.

Perhaps the best way to appreciate the impact of extreme monetization is to go back to the uncool, old economy sector of pizza delivery.

In the 2010s, to try to break a stalemate with its archrival Pizza Hut, Domino's Pizza made a massive investment in digital innovation. The investment was guided by the company's new mission to make ordering via any platform—phone, text, website, email, even by using emoji—easy. By 2015, Domino's was receiving half of its U.S. orders via digital methods; by 2020 that number would grow to 65 percent. Domino's outpaced the competition at mining customer data and communicating tracking details. If a customer had a history of ordering pizza on Friday nights, at 4:00 Friday she might get a text alert offering to deliver a discounted large pie to her door at 6:00. After the customer replied to place an order, she'd get text updates at every step. "It's ordered, it's prepared, it's in the oven, it's ten minutes away, it's five minutes away."

The company also embraced social media early on, using Facebook and Twitter to project authenticity and solicit candid feedback. In one campaign, Domino's asked customers to take a picture of a delivered pizza to show how the actual product compared to what was advertised. A small percentage of pizzas were flops, and Domino's owned up to them. In one case they reached out to a customer in Minnesota and publicly apologized to him for his bad pizza, which became the company's second-best performing commercial ever.

By creating digital feedback loops, Domino's sourced new ideas from customers, built up customer loyalty, and solved problems instead of trying to cover them up with PR. The result: tremendous growth in market share, leaving Pizza Hut in the dust by 2018. Investors rewarded Domino's with a stock price surge from $4 to $305 over ten years—better than most of the tech giants.

A happy ending? No, because in the age of extreme capitalism, every victory is just the prelude to the next war. Even though Domino's managed an A+ digital transformation in the 2010s, it now faces a new existential threat. The enemy is no longer Pizza Hut; it's the new wave of food delivery companies like Uber Eats and DoorDash which are moving into its sector. Very few customers order pizza more than once a week, but millions order three to five times a week from DoorDash, Grubhub, or Uber Eats. While these food delivery "aggregators" don't own their own kitchens, they *do* own the customer experience. They can analyze tons of customer data on food preferences and price elasticity. When food delivery companies partner with "ghost kitchens"—commercial facilities that prepare meals from different cuisines (such as Chinese, Thai, Indian, *and* pizza) from a single physical location, but with different online brands—these delivery companies become even more powerful DDDNs. The Domino's Pizzas of the world are about to get their butts kicked!

It's no wonder that food delivery aggregators and ghost kitchens have raised more than $2 billion in venture capital in the last few years. Privately held DoorDash went public on December 9th, 2020 with a valuation of $32 billion, compared to Domino's market cap of $10.4 billion. New duopolies and DDDNs like DoorDash and Uber Eats are backed by patient venture capital, giving them a huge advantage over Domino's, which is at the mercy of the stock market whenever it has a bad quarter. My firm estimates that the food delivery aggregators are already knocking about 2 to 3 percent off of Domino's annual growth rate. But unless the company takes dramatic action soon in response to these new competitors moving into its lane, its stock price might drop back to $4 in another decade. Or perhaps $0.

What lessons should we draw from this story?

There's no long-term loyalty. Customers will trade loyalty for convenience, for value, or for status. Which means that every company must constantly reevaluate its business and monetization model and value proposition. Otherwise it's easy to win one war but lose the next. In a world of extreme monetization, your business model may be disrupted by a DDDN's monetization model that appears out of nowhere.

The Rise of Duopolies

The emergence of DDDNs and the irrational investing pattern that has decimated traditional companies' ability to compete against them—or to avoid being swept up as DDDNs engage in extreme monetization—has ushered in a new age of duopolies. If you thought consolidation was relentless over the past decade, with mega-mergers like AT&T and Time Warner or Heinz and Kraft, just wait. My firm predicts that more than 90 percent of the current Fortune 500 will be merged, acquired, or go bankrupt by 2050 in deals that will add up to quadrillions of investment capital. The rich (measured in capital, customers, technology, talent, and data) will get richer, and everyone else will have to scrounge for scraps.

When the smoke clears, we can expect to see about a hundred dominant players in about fifty distinct markets, known as value chains, around the world. In most cases there will be a duopoly of two giants in each market. The concepts of banking, financial services, and insurance will converge. Consolidation of telecom, entertainment, and tech will accelerate. Manufacturing, consumer goods, distribution, and retail will merge. Healthcare, pharma, and the public sector will collapse into its own value chain.

Don't expect these duopolies to be equally strong. The first company to establish a DDDN will usually apply its first mover advantage to take 45 to 50 percent of the total addressable market (TAM). A second, more reactionary player will take 20 to 25 percent of the TAM. The remaining 30 percent, give or take, will go to small players who find ways to survive, but who have no hope of catching up to the giants.

These giants will be powered by a long-term focus, access to patient capital pools, and exponential technologies that accelerate their innovation and transformation efforts. They will build vertically integrated data aggregation models, meaning these DDDNs will capture valuable data at all parts of the value chain—from acquisition to partnerships—allowing them to gain deeper and richer data on emerging trends. Using AI, duopolies will uncover new insights to improve customer experience, streamline operations, forecast success of new products, and identify competitors' weaknesses.

Step by step, duopolies will gain economies of scale and drive down the cost of increasing active users. They will increase the time those users spend inside the DDDN—generating even more data, and growing revenue per user. Duopolies will aggregate capital, talent, and curated data to dominate their markets. They will also craft emotional appeals that transcend their respective brands and reflect bigger purpose. In other words, they'll move from delivering on brand promises to activating massive market movements.

How to Compete in the Age of Duopolies

So how can your company thrive in the age of duopolies? You have two options—to become one or to form a coalition with other companies to compete against them.

Option 1: Transform your enterprise into a digital duopoly and become one of the lucky few that emerges victorious in the next five to ten years. It won't be easy, but it is doable. You'll need to:

1. **Balance technology innovation with business model innovation.** You'll need to muster your company's resources, willpower, and ingenuity to create a DDDN. Recruiting and retaining a team of innovators who can create and execute new technology that will power this new DDDN will be critical. Equally important, you'll need to recruit creative business strategists to come up with novel, data-driven business models that can dethrone incumbents. Better tech alone won't lead you to a position of dominance. Your team will need to see the big picture—the nuanced interplay of your technology, business model, target customers, and value

offering. IBM Food Trust is a great example of this approach, using blockchain to deliver business model innovation.

2. **Pursue data supremacy.** It's impossible to overstate the importance of amassing big data as your #1 asset in building a digital duopoly. Without a business model that generates huge amounts of data at every decision point, you're dead on arrival. Companies won't survive the next decade if they continue to fly blind, making intuitive decisions about products, pricing, marketing strategies, and so on. Big data is the key to continuous improvement of your customer experience and operational efficiencies. But just collecting data isn't enough. You also need the intelligence—both human and artificial—to interpret it and apply it wisely. AI, in particular, will need to play a big role in predicting demand for your new products and spotting weaknesses in your competitor's offerings, driving the virtuous cycle of growing your user base while decreasing costs, over and over. One example of this business is Seattle-based EagleView, a startup using drones to capture map data to transform the insurance and business continuity market.

3. **Embrace "benevolent dictator" governance.** It's nice to imagine running a company as a sort of democracy, with every key decision debated and then voted on by all employees. Or perhaps as a "council of elders," with the wisest minds assembled for a constant re-evaluation of strategy. But in the age of duopolies, those are unaffordable luxuries. In companies both big and small, strategic adjustments need to be made quickly, and everyone needs to get on board to execute those changes. My research has shown that to succeed in building a powerful DDDN with long-term strategy, your best bet is to embrace a "benevolent dictator" governance—but only if it empowers the right dictators. The most effective tend to be

owner-operators—i.e., startup founders—who hold onto a controlling equity stake. They have a natural incentive to focus on long-term dominance and stick to the core strategy during a tough quarter. They also have the clout to resist pressure from the board, institutional investors, Wall Street analysts, and media pundits. Alternatives to founders may include private equity firms that can acquire a controlling stake and then execute a disciplined, long-term plan.

Option 2: If you can't build your own duopoly, join a coalition of smaller players in your industry that can collaborate on creating a DDDN. These coalitions will play an increasingly important role in enabling competition against the digital monopolies and duopolies. One fascinating case now in progress is Microsoft's attempt to challenge Amazon through partnerships with retailers like Walmart, Walgreens, and Kroger. These retailers compete with each other, but Amazon is the existential threat they all have in common—giving them an incentive to share cloud computing, advertising networks, and new retail technologies.

In the global shipping business, IBM and Maersk have teamed up to craft a DDDN known as TradeLens, which has led Oracle and Cosco to respond with their own competing coalition, the Global Shipping Network. In the book business, consider the success of the American Booksellers Association, a coalition of independent local bookstores that has survived the rise of Amazon's near-monopoly in online bookselling. The ABA offers its member stores all sorts of digital initiatives, including the Indiebound website, to give local stores access to nationwide sales data, best practices, and economies of scale. Those stores are basically collaborating on their own DDDN, which helps them satisfy their customers and improve their operational inefficiencies. The coalition is giving local bookstores a fighting chance to survive.

· · ·

My research suggests that most organizations will choose option two—to partner with others to build a DDDN—to get started. But, sadly, many will not make the investments in resources and money necessary to succeed. A few market leaders and fast followers will jointly invest. Only a handful will craft and orchestrate their own DDDN and rise to a digital duopoly on their own.

In the chapters that follow, we will explore in detail both of these options. I will show you what strategies to apply when choosing either of them, and how to design your strategic plan to beat the odds and thrive in a world where DDDNs power the post-digital future and duopolies reign.

What about option three, you may be wondering? Can I choose to quietly run my business in my small niche, without the backing of a DDDN and without provoking the giants? The answer, I'm sorry to say, is no. If you want to survive for another decade, there is no other choice. Like it or not, the only options are to build your own duopoly, join a coalition that can hold its own against the dominant DDDNs in your market, or give up and wait for the grim reaper.

Disruption and Destruction

Before we start looking more closely at how to approach options one and two, I'd like to end with a word of caution. While the massive rise of digital duopolies will foster the next wave of disruption and innovation, it will also leave behind a path of destruction. Why? Digital duopolies will usher an era of superefficient yet extreme capitalism.

Duopolies will maximize their operational efficiencies. They will aim to create frictionless transactions—e.g., a transaction so easy that you may not need to hand a credit card or interact with a person. They will aim for massive automation and will try hard

to build autonomous enterprises. Left unchecked, the rise of duopolies can usher a very dark and dystopian winner-takes-all
market that quashes innovation and competition, eliminates a
substantial number of jobs, and leads to a failure of the free market as we know it.

Policymakers and responsible organizations building duopolies must take steps to keep fair competition alive. Success will
require the public and private sectors to team up with foundations to secure and fund the infrastructure, governance, and enforcement mechanisms required to ensure a democratized, fair,
and free market. Successful duopolies will have to abide by
guidelines that require:

1. Open technology standards that prevent market lock-in and
   integration capabilities.

2. Access rights that ensure smaller players can compete on their
   own merits without being duly excluded.

3. Personal data ownership to ensure users have control over
   consent and usage of their personal information, transaction
   history, and other metadata.

With these safeguards in place, duopolies can play an important role in creating super-efficient approaches to building tremendous value to all network participants and creating
opportunities to participate in a rapidly growing and extremely
dynamic network model.

2

THRIVING IN A WORLD OF DIGITAL GIANTS

For a digital giant, rising to become a duopoly is a monumental achievement. After decades of battling old competitors and upstarts—and legal battles with governments along the way—a company that reaches this pinnacle gains significant advantages. Since it is one of two dominant competitors, consumers have fewer choices and their purchase decisions are quick—generating higher profits for the duopolies in the process. When they achieve duopoly status, organizations also tend to spend less money on breakthrough new products, instead addressing incremental innovation and continuing to refine quality and reduce cost. Duopolies gain more time to develop higher-quality offerings less frequently.

There are very few disadvantages when you are a duopoly. But if you are a customer or a potential challenger, a duopoly market can be devastating. In a duopoly market, new entrants, startups, and smaller players face significant barriers to entry. If a market or segment shows growth potential, the duopolies will do everything in their power to intimidate a competitor and even character-assassinate that competitor's brand. From competing on price or underpricing similar offerings, to hostile takeovers or cutting off suppliers, duopolies will gang up to apply significant pressure on any company that challenges them.

In a highly competitive market, competitors often choose to differentiate their brand promise, their positioning, and their offering. But duopolies reduce the number of choices customers may have. And the effort to differentiate their offering is minimal. It's not long before those companies that achieve duopoly status begin to drift off into a sea of complacency. They struggle with innovation: Less competition means less focus on customer success and less investment into new products and innovation. Weak offerings often plague these markets, along with inelastic pricing. Lack of competition keeps prices high and quality lower. After all, duopolies can charge what they want on prices or control supply and availability.

In this chapter, we'll take a look at how duopolies operate, particularly when it comes to pricing, one of the key variables in the dynamics between two firms in a duopoly market. As they do everything in their power to squash competitors, duopolies often walk a fine line when it comes to fair play. If you are an organization looking to partner with others to mount a challenge against digital giants in a duopoly market, understanding how duopolies maintain dominance is critical, as is knowing what practices, regulations, and policies to advocate for to ensure free market competition and fair access.

How Duopolies Compete Today

Traditional models of duopolies cover three major theories based on pricing and supply. Duopolies are a specific type of oligopolies where two organizations control a significant portion of market share, profits, and revenues in a market. In a duopoly, the actions of one organization significantly impact the actions of the other player. You would assume that the two rivals would work out a win-win market to preserve their self-interest. However, duopolies often fall prey to the Prisoner's Dilemma: Acting in their own self-interest, they create an outcome that leaves them both worse off. Why? When both parties choose to protect themselves instead of growing the market or acting in the best interests of the customer, both players get hurt.[1] Based on a game theory originally designed in 1950 by Merrill Flood and Melvin Dresher of the RAND corporation, the paradox shows why two rational parties may choose not to cooperate with each other, even if doing so would be mutually beneficial. Instead, to win at all costs, both parties may be incentivized to cheat and focus on self-interest.

The three most common models of how traditional duopolies compete are the Cournot, the Bertrand, and the Chamberlin models. In the Cournot duopoly model, named after French mathematician Augustin Cournot, companies compete on how much product (or services) they produce. Every production decision by one firm creates an equal response from the other, maintaining an equilibrium in market share and therefore competitive pricing.[2] The Bertrand duopoly model, named after another French mathematician, Joseph Louis François Bertrand, takes an opposite approach. In this model, rival organizations focus on pricing, not output, as the key driver of competition. The Bertrand model assumes that customers will more than likely choose lower-priced goods and services—provided they are of similar quality and have the same features. Should their offerings be equivalent, companies will engage in a price war to win.[3] Finally, in the Chamberlin duopoly model, named after American economist Edward Chamberlin, the two most important variables are the optimum quantity a player should produce and the prices set by each player. Chamberlin's model takes a stance where the two players do not collude but adjust based on self-interest.[4]

These duopoly models, however, don't quite work in the age of digital giants. Whereas traditional duopolies involve companies that can produce a finite supply, digital giants' output is often infinite and not perishable. If you make business software, design a digital avatar, or create a video game, you have the ability to produce an infinite supply of them. With infinite supply and varying degrees of competition (e.g., geographic and cultural bounds, vertical industry constraints, size of business), digital rivals in a duopoly have greater control over their pricing models than the non-digital companies Cournot, Bertrand, and Chamberlin had in mind when they came up with their duopoly models.

These pricing models are massively dynamic, and built-from-the-ground-up digital giants can immediately adjust them. They have a lot more control over pricing and supply than joint venture startups do. Since they are vertically integrated, they do not have to rely on partners to deliver gaps in capability and agree on sourcing terms. For this reason, joint venture startups need to work slightly harder to ensure that the cost structure of production is fully optimized. The key comparison metrics will be profit per sale, return on equity, and percentage market growth. Profit per sale will help partner-led digital giants understand where they need to reduce their cost structure to compete. Return on equity shows how effective investments are as a whole, not just in some parts of the business. Percentage market growth aligns all the partners on gaining market share.

Built-from-the-ground-up digital giants realize that a thriving ecosystem is needed to bring innovation to their networks. That's why they bring in partners that can provide offerings that will reduce the cost to produce and monetize digital goods and services—but digital giants never make them equal partners, so much as suppliers. As with traditional duopolies, digital duopolies must compete for suppliers and attract them into the digital giant's ecosystem. However, built-from-the-ground-up digital giants have tighter control of their channel. They often dictate the rules of access, monetization, and distribution via platforms and marketplaces. Those rules enable them to exert more impactful control by determining the customer experience, pricing, security, and mitigation of channel conflict.

How Apple and Google Vie for Digital Apps Dominance

The battle between the Apple App Store and the Google Play Store is a great example of two digital giants duking it out for dominance in the estimated $402 billion (by 2025) mobile apps market. The competition is not a traditional head-to-head battle over pricing. The battle is over who can attract a healthy ecosystem of innovation partners or suppliers to build their IP in their app stores.

In this digital duopoly, Android has more than six times the market share of users for their operating system than Apple does. Google Android's market share hovers between 85 and 87 percent with Apple at a mere 13 to 15 percent.[5] One could say Google's Android has a monopoly based on market share. Yet, Apple dominates in *revenue* on a scale of two to one, with $32.8 billion in the first half of 2020 compared to Google Pay App Store's $17.3 billion in the first half of 2020.[6] So market share determined solely by the number of mobile operating system users apparently doesn't tell the full story. While Google's Android devices are everywhere, Apple monetizes its phones and digital services much better and is the dominant revenue player.

In 2019, the Apple ecosystem generated $519 billion in economic value. Their physical goods and services drove $419 billion in total revenue, with general retail at $268 billion, travel at $57 billion, and ride hailing at $40 billion. On the digital goods and services front, Apple delivered $61 billion in revenue from the App Store for streaming services, subscriptions, eBooks, classes, and games. Over $45 billion was generated in in-app advertising.[7] Apple owes its success to attracting the top developers to build on its ecosystem. Moreover, Apple keeps a 30 percent commission on all sales supported by its App Store ecosystem from third parties. Over 85 percent of total billing and sales come from the App Store ecosystem, not Apple's own efforts.

Meanwhile Google Play Store also keeps 30 percent of all revenue and, by the numbers, it leads Apple in every category (e.g., number of users, number of apps) other than sales. Given its broad market penetration, Google should be ahead in sales too. Google's ecosystem does have more apps. As of October 2020, Google Play has 2.56 million apps while Apple only has 1.85 million apps.[8] But somehow the Apple ecosystem has attracted top shelf developers and a larger group of customers who pay for their apps.

Also, Apple has simply done a better job of compensating developers. From 2008 until January 2019, developers have earned over $155 billion from software sales.[9] Android developers just make less or in many cases very little. Why? The strong ad-based model that allows free apps usage on Google works great for user adoption but not monetization by developers and content creators. However, Apple's non-ad-based subscriber model favors the developer's ability to generate revenue. Even with the substantial lead of Android phones like Samsung in the market, Apple has won the monetization war by creating favorable conditions for the content creator—not the consumer—including curating a customer base that is used to paying for digital goods and services in exchange for no advertising. As it turns out, success in this duopoly market comes down to building a business model that favors monetization by the developer ecosystem versus a model that provides free access to ad-supported apps, and often generates minimal monetization.

In a digital duopoly the old rules do not apply, as infinite apps can be created and pricing models range from free to full freight.

What Apple's success in the app wars suggest is that digital giants that master the ability to build alliances, coalitions, and partnerships can and will win. The digital giants that can strike a balance between content creator profits and buyers' needs will operate successful marketplaces. Joint venture digital giants *should* have the advantage over built-from-the-ground-up digital giants given that building coalitions and win-win partnerships is part of their DNA.

Extreme Capitalism Emerges Amidst an Age of Duopolies

As the digital giants battle it out and lead to the massive rise of digital duopolies, we can expect the next wave of disruption, innovation, and efficiency. But we will also see a massive path of destruction. Why? Digital duopolies will usher a wave of super-efficient yet extreme capitalism. As companies increasingly are able to reach the end consumer directly, the need for an intermediary will go away. As they automate transactions, much of the manual work of front-line employees and first-line managers will be eliminated. Systems that automatically address regulation will also reduce the manual overhead associated with burdensome regulations. What lies ahead in the age of duopolies is the exponential reduction of non-value-added jobs, decreased market competition, and massive concentration of power and wealth in the hands of a few. By nature, these conditions will increase the likelihood of failure in the free market—unless we put in the right controls and regulatory framework and foster able competitors. Yes, digital giants will create more economic value and consumer benefits due to their size, scale, and reach; but we must also understand the cost of those benefits in order to ensure free markets.

To successfully battle built-from-the-ground-up digital giants, joint venture digital giants will have to take a special role in enabling and ensuring a competitive marketplace. As challengers to build-from-the-ground-up digital giants, they must seek third party assistance from private enterprises, the public sector, and philanthropic institutions to properly secure and fund the critical infrastructure—the regulations and policies—required to ensure a democratized, fair, and free market. They must propose and secure the most minimal but effective legislation, regulation, and outside oversight where possible. This type of regulation and policies will help them emerge as competitors or challengers but will also set the stage for equitable access and free markets in the age of digital giants.

The foundation for this critical shared infrastructure will emerge from a combination of these five impactful policies:

OPEN TECHNOLOGY STANDARDS DEVELOPMENT

Open technology standards play a key role in enabling a growing ecosystem. An open technology standard is a standard that is publicly available and can be used freely by all parties. The "openness" of the technology standard refers to how the standard is created, the broad availability of the specification details, the freely accessible ownership rights, and the ability of the technology to operate across different ecosystems. In many cases, open technology standards preclude fees for use. The goal of standards bodies is to ensure standards can be adopted and implemented on a royalty-free basis in as many markets as possible.

One of the most famous technology standards is TCP/IP, the protocol used for internet communications maintained by the Internet Engineering Task Force (IETF). Created by Vinton G. Cerf and Robert Kahn at Stanford, the Transmission Control Protocol (TCP) and Internet Protocol (IP) are the network communication protocols that enable all the networks of the internet and every device on the internet that supports TCP/IP to communicate.[10] IP is the addressing system of the internet, while TCP provides guaranteed delivery and serialization of data. This open technology standard is shared across an entire ecosystem and no one company or country has a lock on it. The 5G standard for wireless communications is another example of an open technology standard, where global institutions come together to set an industry standard for license to create interoperability.

MARKET ACCESS

Preserving "access rights to markets," especially the marketplaces built by digital giants, ensures that all players in the ecosystem can participate in a fair market. While these marketplaces are proprietary and belong to private companies—the digital giants—they raise concerns when the operators of these marketplaces are also vendors in that marketplace, selling advertising, products, services, memberships, or subscriptions. In the Android and iOS marketplaces, both Apple and Google can write apps that compete with those created by third parties. In ecommerce, Amazon often competes against other sellers with their own branded merchandise. The inherent conflict of interest that emerges when the operator is also a competitor raises a red flag for many regulators. As new markets are created, for example in energy trading or autonomous vehicle networks, proactive governments may step in to design, build, operate, and maintain the actual marketplace and network. Joint venture digital partners have a role in potentially advocating for neutral third parties to operate these networks in order to ensure market access by all players, even competitors.

VALUE EXCHANGE FOR DATA

Data is the heart of every digital giant's business model. And personal data is at the heart of critical infrastructure as well—in a very different way. Today, data is owned by digital giants. But to ensure a fair and free market, our approach to who owns this personal data, how that personal data is used, when that personal data be can used, and what value exchange is provided for it needs to shift. One option is to create a consent framework that enables individuals to take control of their personal data. By extending existing property rights laws to personal data, individuals could then determine whom they want to share what data with, when, for how long, and in exchange for how much value. In the case of healthcare data, a patient might have a wide range of options, from deciding not to share her data, to receiving a one-time compensation for participating in a prospective drug trial, to volunteering her data for use with a charity.

ENFORCEMENT AGENCIES

As duopolies emerge, enforcement agencies must attract top talent and appropriate funding to identify when digital giants cross the line and harm free markets. While these enforcement agencies should never handicap success, especially strong business models, they should proactively determine when consumers may be harmed, challengers may be unfairly treated, and competition stifled. These agencies should encourage innovation through competition and not stifle innovation via regulation.

The counterbalance to enforcement is understanding the impact of regulations on the cost of business and on consumers. For example, the policies of an economic union to protect commoditized jobs may limit the growth of large companies and hurt their ability to drive down the cost of commoditized services in businesses that are competing globally on scale. Consequently, oversight policies should be put in place to analyze existing regulations and understand their economic effect on job creation, national competitiveness, funding of innovation, and risk to national security.

ACTIVATING NONPROFITS AND INDUSTRY COALITIONS

In the same way as think tanks can provide policy capabilities, nonprofits and industry coalitions can play a significant role in serving as the equalizer in enabling competition against digital duopolies. By building stronger nonprofits, open source communities, and industry associations, these institutions can play a role in setting standards, funding innovation, and potentially creating nonprofit arbiters and even competitors. Funded by sovereign wealth funds, family offices, institutional investors, and nonprofit foundations, these entities ensure that both policy and practice enable a fair playing field by researching potential impacts. On one front, these joint venture startups may evolve into the second digital giant in the duopoly. On the other hand, they can provide significant input into any governmental oversight frameworks for competition. Building out third party institutions should be a priority for policymakers.

Looking for Anti-Competitive Practices

In the age of duopolies, both built-from-the-ground-up digital giants and joint venture digital giants will experience a high level of scrutiny for potential marketplace abuses. In highly regulated markets such as the EU, market dominance is defined as having more than 39.7 percent market share. In many cases the EU does consider market share in addition to other factors, such as buyer power, barriers to entry, and market share development over time. But while the percentage thresholds for what constitutes market dominance may change, how dominance is defined will play a significant role in identifying digital giants that have the power to abuse their market position. As we saw in the Google Android versus Apple iOS example earlier in the chapter, market share alone does not necessarily convey market dominance. In the future, market dominance might be defined as the percentage of paid users, or percentage of total transactions, or percentage of personal data controlled, or percentage of economic value created.

Once a digital giant is deemed a dominant company, regulators and politicians seeking to create a more fair playing field should look out for these anti-competitive practices:

- **Forced upsell or cross-sell (tying).** When a company requires that the purchase of one product or service be made with the sale of another to restrict consumer choice. For instance, you want to purchase a video game and you are forced to buy the augmented reality headset with it whether you need it or not.

- **Bundling.** Similar to forced upsell or cross-sell, when a supplier will only sell products that are put into a combined package and will not sell the individual item. For example, you are required to purchase an extended digital warranty for each digital product you buy.

- **Collusion and price fixing.** When competitors work together to pre-determine and agree to either set, increase, or lower prices to impact the market. Imagine every digital mortgage broker got together to agree that they will charge no commission below 2.5 percent. In this case, fixing the floor in pricing would be a form of collusion.

- **Exclusive dealing.** When a customer must purchase a majority or all of a particular type of good or service from a company and is excluded from purchasing from its competitors.

One example would be when a hospital is forced to buy only one brand of hardware to run a type of healthcare software, even though the software could run perfectly on any device.

- **Exclusive rebates**. Plans or loyalty programs that force a customer to purchase the majority or all their goods or services from one company and prevents them from purchasing from a competing one in order to receive a discount. An example of an exclusive rebate would be if one vendor provides rebates and volume discounts only if the customer makes all their purchases exclusively through that vendor.

- **Margin squeezing.** When an integrated firm sells a product that is an essential input at a downstream rival for a similar price as the integrated firm's finished product in order to hamper the rival's ability to survive or compete. For instance, a software vendor that resells its component code to competitors as well as builds its own software on the same code, decides to increase the price of the component code it charges competitors but charges its own internal teams less.

- **Predatory pricing.** When a dominant entity reduces prices that create market side losses in order to force competitors out of a market. For example, a digital giant offers free shipping and returns for purchases at a loss to increase the cost of business for a competitor.

- **Price discrimination.** When some market participants are arbitrarily charged higher prices unrelated to the actual costs of supplying, creating, or distributing the service or good. Charging small businesses one price for a product and large enterprises a higher price without regard for how much volume they order could be considered a price discrimination violation.

- **Refusal to provide IP.** When a dominant firm refuses to license critical intellectual property to potential competitors. An example would be if a critical security technology is banned for use in a competitor's product, leaving them vulnerable to security attacks.

- **Refusal to supply.** Similar to the refusal to provide IP, when a dominant firm limits access to a competitor with a good or service to eliminate competition.

Encouraging Innovation through Antitrust Laws

One of the negative consequences of a duopoly market for consumers is that they block competitors from gaining critical mass. In the course of a challenger's life cycle, leading digital giants will try to partner, acquire, or otherwise threaten it with retaliatory measures. The result? Each value chain will be left with only a couple of digital giants and very small players in niche markets.

In order to encourage competition, governments must enforce antitrust laws that ensure a free-market system and corporations must respect these laws. In the U.S., three pieces of legislation form the core of our antitrust laws. The Sherman Antitrust Act sets rules to prevent restraint of trade or the conspiracy to restrain trade. Fines for violating these rules include up to $100 million for organizations and $1 million for individuals along with up to ten years of imprisonment. The Clayton Antitrust Act regulates mergers and acquisitions, pricing, discounts, and other unfair practices that reduce competition and enable the creation of monopolies. The Federal Trade Commission Act bans all unfair or deceptive acts or practices and unfair methods of competition.

In the U.S. the Federal Trade Commission (FTC) plays a

significant role in supporting free and open markets through competition. The creation, adoption, and enforcement of these rigorous antitrust rules allows for vigorous competition on the merits of a company's offerings. Antitrust rules often remove the impediments to economic opportunity and power economic growth. Without these laws, consumers would face limited access to products and services and would pay higher prices for goods and services. Some of the common antitrust rules involve the prevention of bid rigging, market allocation, mergers and acquisitions, and price fixing:

BID RIGGING

Preventing bid rigging—bid suppression, bid rotation, and cover bidding—requires vigilance. This illegal practice allows companies to predetermine who will win a bid by having a number of parties make intentionally weak bids on a contract just to ensure that the predetermined winner gets it. For example, competitors might collude to withdraw bids or refrain from bidding until the designated winner's bid is accepted (bid suppression). Or colluders might submit unacceptably high bids with no-go conditions to provide the illusion of a fair auction (cover bidding). Or competitors might take turns being the lowest bidder and winning the contract (bid rotation).

MARKET ALLOCATION

Market allocation is a scheme among competitors to divide markets by customer type, geography, size, or industry for the purpose of controlling pricing. In 2001, the FTC found FMC Corp. guilty of colluding with Asahi Chemical Industry to divide global markets for microcrystalline cellulose, a key ingredient in pharmaceutical tablets. FMC was banned from distributing their offering to any competitors until 2011 as well as any Asahi products until 2016.[11] Now, imagine if a video streaming service worked with competitors to collude on what content they would each make available in which regions. This would be an example of market allocation in an age of digital duopolies.

MERGERS AND ACQUISITIONS

Preventing questionable mergers and acquisitions also plays a key role in enabling competition. Three main scenarios for mergers include horizontal, vertical, and potential competition mergers. Horizontal mergers involve the acquisition of companies that make similar things or companies that distribute similar items. In 2004, the FTC challenged the merger between General Electric and Agfa's non-destructive testing (NDT) business. Given the dominant market share each company held in this area, GE Healthcare had to divest of its Panametric subsidiary's NDT business for the merger to proceed.[12]

Vertical mergers assess the supply chain and ecosystem impact of ownership of companies buying all the different stages of how a product gets produced, distributed, and even serviced. In 2005, Valero Energy had to divest businesses and form an informational firewall in order to acquire two ethanol terminal operators, Kaneb Services and Pipe Line Partners. In this case the FTC feared that post-merger scenarios would provide Valero with an opportunity to cut-off a competitor's access to supplies.[13]

Potential competition mergers challenge pre-emptive mergers that may take out a younger competitor. In 2015, the FTC blocked the Sysco–U.S. Foods merger, a merger of the two largest food distributors in the U.S., that could have led to higher commercial and restaurant food prices.[14]

PRICE FIXING

Price fixing or collusion occurs when competitors agree to set prices outside of market forces. In most cases, price collusion cheats consumers by subjecting them to higher costs. The inverse of this scenario is when a competitor tries to stop challengers from entering a market by lowering the price of their offerings. An oversight group such as the FTC can require a company to divest the rights to build a competing product or service offering if they produce the key ingredient in the supply chain. In 2017, the FTC charged Mallinckrodt $100 million in fines for acquiring a competing pharmaceutical company—the only one that posed a potential challenge to its infant anti-seizure drug—in order to protect the drug's monopoly on the market.[15]

Protecting Digital Giants from Over-regulation

The balance between over-regulation and no regulation is delicate. To achieve it, regulatory bodies have to engage in a cost-benefit analysis. Most regulation is designed to protect the consumer and the smaller competitors. But regulation must also consider the benefits that come from a duopoly market: the stable creation of a new market, increase in the number of jobs, and market efficiencies gained for the consumer. New markets create and expand new categories for spending and for hiring. New types of jobs are created along with new opportunities for both the new market and its ancillary ecosystem. Market efficiencies include cheaper pricing, easier access, and more choices for customers.

In some markets, the minimum efficient scale for a given product, service, or experience is one or two per market—or even per planet. At that point these entities may emerge as regulated duopolies like Airbus and Boeing. They both sell planes, everyone can board them at an airport, and few passengers care what type of plane they are boarding. These factors should be taken into account when considering regulations of digital duopolies.

A key guideline to keep regulation in check is to put the burden of proof on governments to show how an organization's actions or behaviors harm consumers in a market as opposed to measuring how a policy change *may* improve competition. For example, dominant streaming services built on membership and advertising revenue may end up creating new models that disrupt traditional cable, satellite, and movie theater distribution. The net result is that consumers will pay less per view, content creators and consumers will avoid massive distribution fees, and more money will go back to the content creator. These benefits could outweigh the fact that there are only two streaming players with a dominant market share, and that more expensive traditional competitors are being disrupted in the market.

The European Union provides some clear guidelines under Article 102 for their Court of Justice on how dominant firms may justify defense of alleged market abuses. The framework asks the dominant company to show that any resulting negative consequences from their actions are outweighed by the efficiencies promoted. The European Union Commission's *Guidance* states that four cumulative conditions must be satisfied:

1. The efficiencies would have to be realized, or be likely to be realized, as a result of the conduct.

2. The conduct would have to be indispensable to the realization of those efficiencies.

3. The efficiencies would have to outweigh any negative effects on competition and consumer welfare.

4. The conduct must not eliminate all effective competition.[16]

The successful balance between growth and regulation will require a deft hand and smart regulators. The massive influence of digital giants on politics, society, and the economy require the smartest and most skilled professionals to ensure that policies not only address the policy needs of today, but also builds in a futurist view of the impact today's polices may have for generations to come.

3

BUSINESS UNUSUAL:
THE AGE OF DUOPOLIES

Over the past decade, digital transformation has evolved from being the "new thing" in business to "business as usual." Before COVID-19, business leaders faced massive pressure to not only embark, but also complete their companies' digital journeys. Most were either trying to play catch up to startups that had come out of nowhere to disrupt their industries or to existing competitors who had gotten an earlier start at digital transformation. Since these leaders had no margin for error, they tried to find a playbook or blueprint to show them exactly how to execute their digital transformation strategies. They sought case studies and examples of successful companies they could model, anticipating their boards' reaction to the digital transformation plans they were considering: "Has this been done before? Where?" Of course, these boards were missing the point.

Organizations traditionally have prioritized their strategy and budgets according to the "business hierarchy of needs." Remember Maslow's hierarchy of needs? This theory, which seeks to define the needs that motivate us, suggests that, at the very basic level, we are driven by our physiological needs for air, food, water, shelter, and so on. At the next level, we are driven by our need for safety (i.e., feeling safe, having a secure job, being healthy, having enough resources). From there, the next two levels up focus on our need for belonging and love (e.g., from our relationships, friends, society) and the need for esteem (feeling accomplished, respected, achieving status, having freedom or agency, and so on). The top level is characterized by our need for self-actualization, where individuals achieve their full potential and also self-awareness.

The business version of the hierarchy of needs also has five levels. The base level is the need to be in sound regulatory compliance. The goal? To keep everyone safe by following the rules and avoiding risk. The second level of needs is operational efficiency. The goal at this level is to ensure the operation is running smoothly and as lean as possible: focus on cost savings, improvements in throughput, and automation. The third level of needs is a focus on revenue and growth (e.g., selling motions, pricing strategies, indirect channels, and new offerings). The fourth level is business model transformation. At this level, organizations focus on improving and optimizing both their monetization models and business models. Brand caps off the top of the hierarchy, when organizations zero in on clearly defining their mission and purpose to align with their brand actions.

In the business hierarchy of needs, business executives have traditionally focused first on regulatory compliance and operational efficiency. Finding ways to mitigate risk and save money always seems easier than growing the business. So instead of going for bold digital transformation initiatives, most boards and their complicit executives opted for smaller projects that typically solved . . . regulatory compliance issues and improved operational efficiency. Bird in hand, they said!

It's not like these companies were equipped to do much more than that: Most of their executive teams lacked the skillsets to drive organic growth and invest for long-term innovation, anyway. Instead, they were laser-focused on the short-term, quarter-to-quarter metrics emphasized by their boards. They had gotten accustomed to the same tried and tired MBA playbooks and strategy consultant decks. The result? As they focused on the bottom of the pyramid, only a few companies enjoyed breakthrough and sustainable success.

That's because successful digital transformation requires a fundamental shift from focusing on mitigating risk and operational efficiency to developing a mindset fixed on growing revenue and developing new bold business models. Success requires a complete rethink of the brand. Companies have to ask themselves, "What's our mission and purpose?" "Why do we exist?" They have to differentiate themselves from competitors by crafting new business models. They must sell the right offerings to their customers. What about operational efficiency and regulatory compliance? Sure, these are important, but to effectively transform the company, organizations must automate through software and data much of the work typically done to improve operational efficiency and regulatory compliance. Companies must have their best people focused on the *top* of the pyramid, not on cutting a penny here and there. In short, companies must flip the pyramid (see Figure 3.1).

FIGURE 3.1. ORGANIZATIONS MUST FLIP THE PYRAMID TO JUMPSTART GROWTH.

But today many of us who led full-scaled digital transformation efforts by flipping the pyramid feel that we've achieved only limited success for these herculean efforts. Yes, some of us survived to fight another battle. But the investments we made have proven not enough to succeed in our current business environment. So, what happened? Why did all this effort not result in game-changing transformation? We did all the right things. We transformed business models. We changed engagement. We were supposed to come out winners. And yet only a few of us made it past the finish line.

Suddenly successfully embracing digital transformation was not enough. Our competition was no longer whom we thought it was. Even as direct competitors fall by the wayside and pose less of a threat, competition from nontraditional players continues to increase. In many cases, adjacent value chains compete head on with our companies.

As it turns out, while we were heads down on digital transformation, a very small but clever group of business leaders (helped by investors who took our hard-earned profits to fund startups to compete in our same markets) figured out how to disrupt those of us embarking on digital businesses. They were focused on creating the next big thing. This wasn't a new methodology or a technology shift. This was much more than a new business model. It was a business built on the power of multi-sided networks and massive amounts of data—determined to dominate their markets and, maybe, share the stage with whomever won second place. As the coronavirus hit, swallowing with it thousands of businesses that couldn't survive the economic shutdown that followed, these duopolies simply got bigger and more powerful.

In the wake of COVID-19, duopolies will be more disruptive than any other business force we've seen before. We will simultaneously face a massive crisis and opportunity to reinvent our businesses. But to succeed in this post-pandemic age of duopolies, companies will not be able to engage in "business as usual." Simply embarking in yet another digital transformation won't be enough. First, we will have to examine and avoid the traps that lurk within our corporate cultures, preventing us from engaging in meaningful, substantive change. Then, we'll need to completely rethink how we approach our businesses so they can truly compete in this brave new world.

The Seven Common Traps that Derail Meaningful Transformation

Even in the face of mass disruption, incumbent companies *do* have a chance to catch up to—or even get ahead of—competitors that have managed to get an early start. In fact, many incumbents can take the lead and set the pace for the rest of their industries. But often, the first obstacle they have to overcome is themselves.

Used to viewing the world with short-term lenses, companies and their leaders often fall into traps that prevent their success in any meaningful change effort. Let's start by understanding what derails organizations from meaningful transformation. We can start by identifying seven of the most common traps (see Figure 3.2). Knowing what *not* to do creates room for us to find the right approach forward, allowing us to engage successfully in the huge task of building a duopoly or joining others to form one.

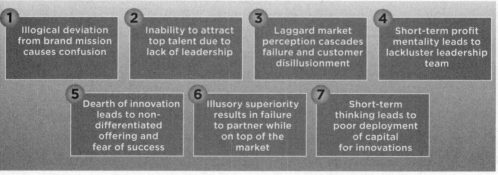

FIGURE 3.2. SEVEN COMMON TRAPS THAT DERAIL
MEANINGFUL TRANSFORMATION.

1. ILLOGICAL DEVIATION FROM BRAND MISSION CAUSES CONFUSION

Companies often extend their brand mission into other product categories or even markets. For example, Avis Rent-a-Car has recently announced its intent to move beyond being just a rental car company to becoming a fleet manager—organizing and coordinating work vehicles for other businesses. The goal—to provide uptime for car availability. Using its data and logistics experience, Avis can optimize vehicle maintenance windows, ensuring their clients will never worry about a truck, car, or other motor vehicle being in the shop when they need it. Leveraging this data allows Avis to shift from a transactional consumer relationship to an experiential business-to-business and outcomes-based relationship. And customers like it. They find Avis's move to fleet manager a reasonable extension of its brand. Avis already leases out a lot of rental cars. Fleet owners find it plausible and possible that Avis can manage vehicles across the value chain from finding the right car, managing and operating the car, and then selling the car at the maximum value when it leaves the fleet.

But when companies try to provide offerings that solve a problem the existing customer feels is too outside the scope of their original brand mission, failure often follows. Three examples of illogical deviation from a brand mission come to mind: Cheetos Lip Balm, Colgate kitchen entrées, and Harley Davidson perfume.[1] In 2005 Pepsi company subsidiary Frito-Lay thought they could use the Cheetos brand—for decades, one of its most popular snacks—to enter the lip balm market against established brands such as ChapStick, Blistex, and Burt's Bees. As you can imagine it was a colossal failure: Snack foods and lip balm just didn't seem to have much in common, so Frito-Lay's move into the personal care market was not seen as a good brand extension.[2]

Another of the world's powerhouse brands thought that they had permission to extend . . . from personal care into prepared foods. Through its extensive consumer research, Colgate Palmolive found that Americans really like frozen meals. Instead of creating a new brand to cater to this consumer need, in 1982 the company introduced Colgate kitchen entrées. What they failed to understand was that when consumers think about Colgate they think about minty toothpaste—not tasty foods.

Finally, in 1994, Harley-Davidson decided it would be a good idea to introduce a female perfume. Never mind that Harley Davidson is more of an iconic masculine brand than a female one. The new perfume did not fly off the shelves. Despite this failure, Harley Davidson kept licensing their brand for other brand extensions such as wine coolers and aftershave. None were successful. All were legendary brand overextension failures.

2. INABILITY TO ATTRACT TOP TALENT DUE TO LACK OF LEADERSHIP

Top talent attracts top talent. "A" players attract "A" players. "B" players attract "C" players. But it all starts at the top. For years, Salesforce.com CEO Marc Benioff sold a vision of "no software" that appealed to the tech community eager to transform the software business model.[3] Today, his "tech for good" message attracts the best and brightest.

Meanwhile, another large tech company was led by a CEO who failed not only to attract top talent but also to retain top talent. This leader changed workforce policies under the guise of a reduction in head count and promoted unqualified individuals under the guise of diversity and inclusion, stripping the ranks of any sense of meritocracy and leading to a brain drain. As talented individuals fled, their replacements were not of the same caliber.

3. LAGGARD MARKET PERCEPTION CASCADES
FAILURE AND CUSTOMER DISILLUSIONMENT

Faced with a declining brand, some companies try to revive it by taking the shortcut of branding without substance—instead of meaningfully redefining their mission and purpose with new business models. When this happens, the brand enters an era of "negative market perception." Facebook has emerged as the poster child for laggard market perception and negative brand. From privacy scandals to botched product rollouts to continued bad press, Facebook has seen its ad growth slow, its customer signups decelerate, and ad rates drop.

As soon as a business is seen as devoid of innovation, peddling a commoditized, nondifferentiated product, all stakeholders—employees, customers, partners, suppliers, and investors—lower their expectations, leading to a focus on short-term gain, declining employee morale, lack of interest by investors, and lower quality from suppliers.

Once the brand has been battered, employees lose a sense of pride and quality often drops. Customers no longer have an affinity for a brand that has sold its soul and won't pay premium pricing when they no longer see value. Salespeople lose their bravado in deals as they lose confidence. Moreover, as customers seek deals more aggressively, the salespeople lose their discipline to hold prices and command larger margins. Other companies lose interest in creating co-innovation and co-creation partnerships with laggards because their credibility in the public eye suffers.

For example, an auto supplier whose client is a premium brand like Tesla will go out of its way to show the innovative electric car company its best products. Granted, the quality this supplier offers Tesla might be the same as what they offer to an internal combustion auto manufacturer, their delivery schedules might be equally aggressively, even cost might even be the same. But this supplier would likely make every effort to reduce friction for a customer they love—and belief is an innovative player in the field—and go out of their way for that customer. In return, Tesla does not have to try hard to win their business. Instead, Tesla can ask for less money, more requirements, and better terms and conditions in order for the supplier to tout their work with the automaker.

4. SHORT-TERM PROFIT MENTALITY LEADS TO LACKLUSTER LEADERSHIP TEAM

Modern leaders must be able to not only articulate the vision and mission of their organizations but also live its values. However, the thread of hostile takeovers and pressure from so called "growth-based" private equity (PE) firms focused on squeezing greater amounts of EBITDA (earnings before interest, taxes, depreciation, and amortization) from companies have led to a generation of "Yes Person" CEOs who create anorexic environments for innovation.

These CEOs emphasize cost cutting to increase share price results—and rarely understand (or surround themselves with those who understand) how to create a culture of sustained innovation and long-term growth. This driving out of innovation and growth hurts organizations in the long run. The playbook for many of these PE-owned firms starts with reducing the overall innovation budget under the guise of reducing product lines while "investing more in each existing product." As the overall R&D investment drops, the management team emphasizes their focus on a few product offerings and concentrate their efforts. Meanwhile, they cut down on marketing and sales expenses to drive down cost of sale. The goal is to move operations to pre-set benchmarks. Most companies that operate under this playbook incur more technical debt as key infrastructure investments are put on hold to favor short-term investment to improve features of the existing products. Over time this catch-22 continues until customers abandon them. Most private equity (PE) led software companies that follow this playbook fail to digital transformation efforts or very ineffective approaches.

One large PE firm, for example, traditionally attracts, hires, and compensates well leaders who just follow the rules, fail to think outside of the box, and often lack a strong moral compass. These CEOs and their leadership teams follow the PE "standard operating procedures," delivering the returns expected by shareholders with no regard to product innovation, minimal concern for customers, and very little thought for employees and their morale.

5. DEARTH OF INNOVATION LEADS TO NONDIFFERENTIATED OFFERINGS AND FEAR OF SUCCESS

Nothing reeks of failure more than a copycat product that arrives a cycle late into the marketplace. Companies that are just doing the bare minimum often have had the EBITDA militants and legal teams dictate product direction. Yes, playing it safe and riding on the remaining vestiges of brand cachet can help a short-term CEO and board hit their targets. But this leaves the company without any differentiation from its competitors, leading to long-term consequences. The U.S. auto industry in the 1980s provides a great case study on how to lose market share when low-cost challengers enter your space. When Japanese automakers entered the U.S. market, U.S. automakers were caught flat-footed. As they had not invested in long-term innovation, they had difficulty competing against the more efficient, reliable, and less expensive cars produced by Toyota, Nissan, Honda, and so on. This led to the eventual loss of market share in small cars, sedans, and light trucks.

If your company's goal is to be the most profitable copycat in your industry, my guess is that this game already has already ended in commoditized markets where the battle for return on equity leaves few players battling a death match with no winners. There are exceptions. For a period of time, South Korean electronics firms managed to take innovations from the Japanese and build bigger, profitable challengers. During the Japanese economic collapse, South Korean companies sat outside the headquarters of Japanese companies offering cash to interview key executives, engineers, and sales professionals for their know-how. Using what they learned, the powerful chaebols clawed their way into markets with waves of copycat features. But over time, they also realized they had to commit to innovation in order to not only grow but to survive market annihilation.

6. ILLUSORY SUPERIORITY RESULTS IN FAILURE TO PARTNER WHILE ON TOP OF THE MARKET

Ego and delusions of grandeur often beset successful market leaders. Thinking that their company knows best and that partners, suppliers, customers, and even competitors have little to offer stifles their growth and transformation efforts. The result? Poor treatment of partners and suppliers, ignoring customer requests, and disregard for emerging opportunities. As their egos take over, some companies believe they can replicate or create whatever one of their partners or competitors has to offer results, failing to understand their limitations and capabilities.

BlackBerry's dominance in the 2000s, for example, came to a standstill due, in large part, to its overall market and leadership hubris. When customers asked for access to video and the internet, the company took too long to respond. The management team simply did not believe the BlackBerry could be displaced by Apple's iPhone, which didn't even have a physical keyboard and was geared toward general consumers, not enterprise customers. Their disbelief that the consumerization of IT had taken off—which they dismissed because the idea was "not invented here" (NIH) in Waterloo, Ontario, compounded Blackberry's demise. Today, one may question whether, despite crushing it on EBITDA and return on capital, Apple still has the innovation chops to survive as product innovations slow, new phones lack key features of competitors, and software introduction remains buggy.

7. SHORT-TERM THINKING LEADS TO POOR DEPLOYMENT OF CAPITAL FOR INNOVATIONS

Decades of cost-cutting, mergers and acquisitions, and activist shareholder fights have crushed the growth and innovation culture at many organizations. This strangulation of capital funding for innovation has decimated legacy enterprises, leaving them vulnerable to attacks by innovative competitors and new entrants in the market. A 2004 and 2005 survey by the Duke Fuqua business school showed that 55 percent of chief financial officers at 400 of America's largest public companies would sacrifice their firm's economic value to meet a quarterly expectation. Rather than investing in equipment for employees, CFOs would rather take the short-term gain and spin the dice for another quarter.[4] This study still holds true today.

The airline industry post-COVID-19 provides the best example of the stripping of innovation funding at major, legacy businesses. Take American Airlines, which filed for bankruptcy in 2011 but became profitable again by 2014. During a six-year period of record profits, the airline failed to put together a rainy-day fund for a crisis. It also failed to modernize its technology systems, aircraft, and operating procedures that would improve digital channels, improve analytics, and develop better planning capabilities. Instead, it spent $12 billion of its positive cash flow since 2014 in stock buybacks. American was not alone in the excessive buybacks: Most of the airlines spent 96 percent of their free cash flow on buybacks from 2010 to 2020.[5]

In order to prepare yourself to compete in the age of duopolies—which will require massive and meaningful change—your company will need to avoid these seven traps. Rising to the threat that duopolies present is not easy. The typical inertia of boards often hinders an organization's ability to change and succeed fast enough. Adopting a level of self-awareness might just provide your company the fighting chance needed to set the stage.

The Five Pillars of Growth and Change

Now that we know what common traps companies must avoid to pull off successful transformation, the next step is understanding that the kind of change required to either become or compete against a duopoly is not business as usual. It's more than a digital transformation; it's more than a turnaround. It's a complete rethink of your business.

In the past, when a company executed a "turnaround," it usually targeted one or two of five focus areas—what I call the five pillars—for transformation: the company's purpose, its team, its offerings, the market in which it competes, and the capital it has at its disposal. For example, a company might focus on the "team" pillar by bringing in a new executive to revamp the talent needed to execute a new initiative. Or leaders might focus on the "offering" pillar by looking to apply an exponential technology to execute its turnaround. Or it might focus on the "markets" pillar by expanding its partner ecosystems. But to mount the kind of change required to create a data-driven digital network that can rise to a duopoly or compete against one, companies will need to radically rethink all five pillars simultaneously.

To do so, leaders should start by studying the five pillars to help them understand the changes they'll need to make in order to create, participate with, and compete against future duopolies (see Figure 3.3). Each pillar has:

- An objective—the aim or purpose of that particular area of focus.
- A metric—how each pillar is measured.
- An initial catalyst—what companies typically focus on within this pillar during the early stages of its life.
- A turnaround catalyst—what's required to reinvigorate the pillar.
- A duopoly strategy—the specific play related to that pillar that will help companies prepare for the future.

LEVEL	1	2	3	4	5
Pillar	Purpose	Team	Offering	Markets	Capital
Objective	Answer the "why." What is the mission?	Attract and retain talent	Deliver a minimum viable offering	Win the top customers in each market	Maximize deployment of capital
Metric	Brand value	Best place to work	Analyst reports	Market share Customer satisfaction	Profit per scale Revenue per employee
Initial catalyst	Dynamic founder	Talent networks	Design	Category kings	Capital flows
Turnaround catalyst	Owner operator	Stock upside	Exponential technology	Partner ecosystems	Refreshing investment cycles
Duopoly strategy	Think bigger	Grow the next level	Iterative customer feedback	Trading networks	Value exchange

FIGURE 3.3. THE FIVE PILLARS OF GROWTH AND CHANGE.

PILLAR ONE: PURPOSE

Every organization must answer the question, *why?* Why does it exist? What is its mission? What is the broader social good it provides? A company's purpose is its north star; it defines the company's values and helps stakeholders understand how the company will behave. You might recognize the "purpose" of some familiar companies. For example, unlike most hotel chains, the Four Seasons' over a hundred locations each have a unique feel despite all manifesting one central brand identity. The three Cs—connection, craftsmanship, and character—are expressed by each hotel, which goes out of its way to represent the local culture, its people, traditions, and design character.

Purpose describes the actions that keep you focused on why you exist. The way we measure whether a company's purpose is doing what it's supposed to do is through its brand value: How much is the brand worth in the marketplace? A strong purpose will manifest in brand loyalty and higher margins. A weak one will show up as a fickle customer base and in a constant reliance on value pricing. Weak purpose results in the worth of the brand being lowered in the eyes of the market. The initial catalyst of a company's purpose is a dynamic founder—the person who created or led the company in its infancy, often taking it from startup to corporation, even to an initial public offering with a clear vision for what they wanted the company to achieve and stand for. In the midst of a turnaround, owner-operators—leaders who have significant financial stakes in the company and majority board control—often play a similar role to a dynamic founder, refocusing the company's purpose, rallying the organization behind it, and reinventing the business. As you rethink how your company's purpose might need to adapt in order to compete in the age of duopolies, think bigger and dream outside the comfort zone of what you believe is possible. Take a moment to study the entire value chain; think about how your company is connected to a web of partners and suppliers who provide a final solution to your customer. Understand your company's internal operations, marketing and sales, customer service, technical development, human resources, procurement, and so on. Identify a purpose that resonates across the value chain. For example, if your company sells mattresses and pillows, your purpose might be "helping people sleep better" like it is for Purple Company or MyPillow. If your company sells thermostats and electronic controls for building management, think bigger and craft a purpose that zeroes in on how you help create smart buildings that drive down energy consumption, reduce downtime and maintenance costs, and improve workers' health.

PILLAR TWO: TEAM

To succeed, your company needs to attract and retain top talent. In the digital world, you want the most motivated and skilled individuals working for you. Having top talent in your ranks allows you to more quickly innovate, go to market, and mitigate risk. Without great talent, you miss out on opportunities, lack empathy for your customer, and fail to learn quickly. A good metric to determine whether you're accomplishing this objective is whether your company consistently earns best-place-to-work ratings from your employees. When employees feel happy, challenged, satisfied, and valued, they stay. By creating great places to work, you not only retain your best people, but attract additional people into these networks. Early on in the life of a company, the catalyst for this pillar is precisely these talent networks—employees who bring the best people from their circles into the company, driving growth through their talent and expertise. But when teams hit a slump, become demoralized, or become the focus of a turnaround boards must create conditions to re-engineer a stock upside for top talent as well non-monetary incentives, enabling them to entice the very best not just for short-term destructive growth but for long-term sustainable growth. As teams age and get settled, companies must focus on bringing in fresh talent to mentor and grow into the next level.

When you are reinventing your company into a dynamic business that can compete head to head with duopolies, there's no room for the inefficiencies and fecklessness of bureaucracy that often hamper legacy organizations. The secret to success comes from implementing "benevolent dictatorship governance"—a dual class A, class B governance structure where the leader is given 10:1 voting rights, allowing them to make strong decisions while bringing along new investors. This approach allows for more shares to be issued to employees and the public while retaining the founders' control over the vision of the company. This governance model has enabled tech giants such as Amazon, Facebook, Google, Oracle, and others to execute a long-term strategy to dominate their markets without having to succumb to every short-term whim from shareholders, activist groups, and investors. Benevolent dictatorships inspire quick action and high-performing teams. Teams know that the decisions made by leaders will not waver and that the leaders have their teams' backs.

This approach enables leaders to strategically map out the ringers—those leaders who inspire others—across the entire talent pipeline and reward them. They know loyalty and performance will be backed up by actions. Often seen as star players, ringers attract key talent through their skills and professional reputation. As each management level is built out, recruiters focus on bringing the high performing "ringers" and the ringers know they will be adequately compensated for their work and that their mission will not be deterred by a level of bureaucratic bullshit.

PILLAR THREE: OFFERING

The main objective of the "offering" pillar is to drive growth through a minimum viable offering. By that, I mean how quickly you can deliver the minimum set of requirements for your customers. For example, the minimum viable offering of Zoom was the ability to place a quick video call with someone without the fuss required to set up a call, find a connection, and then fiddle with adjustments. Once the offering became popular during the pandemic, customers' requirements for security increased, leading Zoom to develop additional features such as waiting rooms, more secure passwords, and virtual backgrounds.

After a company delivers the minimum viable offering, it can focus on product-line extensions that are refined by innovation programs and customer feedback. This customer feedback is used to improve the offering and create additional value and revenue sources. The goal is to win over the critics through analyst reports, influencer recognition, and customer appeal—the metric typically used to determine whether the minimum viable offering was successful.

When a company is young, the initial catalyst for this pillar is design: The minimum viable offering driving growth was designed to fill an unmet market need. But as time passes, the designs that fueled the minimum viable offering and its subsequent extensions no longer meet market needs. But now the company is under the spell of short-term focused shareholders and investors. CFOs and bean counters start dictating product innovation. They look at profit per unit sold. Innovation budgets are reduced and creativity declines. Almost every industry has seen this type of decline as shareholder quest for margin trumps investment in long-term product roadmaps.

When focusing on this pillar during a turnaround, companies

turn to exponential technology—technologies that advance at breakneck speed and have the potential to disrupt how we work and live (e.g., the cloud, the Internet of Things, big data, automation, augmented reality, virtual reality, robotics, blockchain, artificial intelligence, nanotechnology, and quantum computing) to revitalize their offerings. Take the home appliance market, which has turned to exponential technology to breathe new life into its offerings like refrigerators. These devices are increasingly becoming "smart," collecting data and sharing it with their users. Cars connected to the cloud have allowed automakers to create new offerings that support autonomous vehicles. The health industry has relied on 5G, video technology, and robotics to revitalize how it delivers services to patients, through telehealth and robotic surgery, for example. The goal is to use these exponential technologies to transform the offering and make it faster, better, and sometimes cheaper.

As companies rethink their offerings in their quest to become a duopoly or to challenge one, they need to consider how they can build digital feedback loops—where data is collected, analyzed, and applied into new business models—into their offerings and how they can use AI to create iterative feedback over time. These feedback loops can tell them whether customers are happy with the offering or not. They can assess which features are being used and which are not, allowing the company to conduct market testing and reallocate investments based on consumer demand. Feedback loops also help model supply and demand, enabling pricing optimization. Using artificial intelligence to parse this rich consumer data gives companies the capability to rapidly assess, understand, react, and improve their offerings. This valuable data which allows companies to improve decisions about their offerings creates an exponential advantage over the competition.

PILLAR FOUR: MARKETS

The objective of this focus area or pillar is to drive growth by winning the top customers in each market. Traditionally "growing markets" has meant expanding geographically. The goal has been to expand from a few local locations to statewide coverage. Even greater growth comes from expanding from statewide to nationwide presence. Once a company is fully in one country, it might try to expand within the international region, eventually going global. Another type of expansion looks at industry verticals. For example, a company's success in retail may lead to it making a push into the travel and hospitality markets. Another way to grow your markets means pursuing bigger customers. Some companies may go from targeting small- and medium-sized businesses (those under 500 employees and $250 million in revenue) to focusing on companies in the midmarket (those between 500 and 1,000 employees and about $250 million to $1 billion in revenue) or even large enterprise customers (those greater than 1,000 employees and $1 billion in revenue).

Companies must take an account-based approach to target customers who are "market leaders" and "fast followers" in each category in which they compete. While market leaders represent less than 5 percent of companies, they are proactive and transformative. Fast followers embody about 15 percent of companies and are reactive and transformative. Cautious adopters comprise 50 percent of organizations and they are proactive and incremental. Meanwhile, laggards are reactive and incremental and make up 30 percent of organizations. Going after market leaders and fast followers is important because these companies will generally outpace their competitors in growth and acquire laggards and cautious adopters to expand markets, secure their base, or acquire talent.

The top companies attract market leaders and fast followers.

The key indicator of how well a company is doing in this focus area is the size of the market share of early adopters it captures—as well as their satisfaction. When a company is starting out, the catalyst for growth comes from the creation of "category kings," a term made famous by Silicon Valley marketing legend Chris Lochhead.[6] Category kings—companies that create, define, and then dominate a whole new category of business—own markets. For example, DocuSign and EchoSign were category kings in the e-signature market—they created an entire new category of product that didn't exist before.

In order to compete in the age of duopolies, you will need to take your approach to winning markets to a completely different level. The key will be focusing strategically on your partner ecosystem and creating joint venture startups. These startups can renew your company's access to markets by taking advantage of your partner's distribution network and building data-driven digital networks (DDDNs) across a value chain or ecosystem.

PILLAR FIVE: CAPITAL

The "capital" pillar typically comes into play when the organization matures. The focus on capital often begins during the fundraising phase of a startup. Startups seek funding to power their growth and expand into markets. Venture capital funding and early investors provide the initial catalyst. These capital flows provide the lifeblood of the organization and help them achieve "the rule of 40": where a company's combined growth rate and profit margin exceeds 40 percent. Tech startups who achieve the rule of 40 are rewarded with higher valuations and a path to an initial public offering.

In the pre-IPO and post-IPO phases of a company's life, profitability often rises to the top of its priorities. As companies maximize the deployment of capital—that is, they focus on how well they are using their money—the metrics they favor to measure how well they are doing are profit per sales and profit per employee. Both of these benchmarking metrics are used to compare performance among competitors. At some point when growth slows, leaders start to focus on profitability over growth, and short-term quarter-to-quarter decisions dominate mid-term to long-term health. The organization starts to overemphasize capital at the expense of the other four pillars.

Without any emphasis on the four other focus areas, organizations often lose their way with customers. A successful turnaround catalyst is new capital flow that enters the marketplace, disrupting the incumbents. New capital flows allow the organization to rethink its mission and purpose, change leadership, invest in the offering and markets. Sometimes PE firms can provide this turnaround catalyst.

Duopolies require reinvestment in the investment cycle by focusing on value exchange models and not just EBITDA. Simply cutting costs will not lead to growth. The monetization of digital assets will create the value exchange. Leaders focus on new forms of monetary and non-monetary value exchange. Nonmonetary value exchange includes recognition, access, impact, and action. Investment vehicles such as cryptocurrencies, point systems and credits, and other mechanisms provide another form of value exchange.

Leaders of any mature company wishing to compete in the age of duopolies must re-examine their investment in each of these pillars or focus areas and understand the commitment required to jumpstart growth and innovation in a bold way. Because the initial catalyst no longer provides enough momentum for success, leaders and their boards must create the conditions to support a turnaround catalyst in each focus area simultaneously:

The organization's purpose should expand beyond the company's original mission to address the full value chain. The organization should adopt a benevolent dictatorship governance structure. The company's offerings should build-in AI-driven digital feedback loops. The organization should apply data-driven digital networks (DDDNs) to win markets. And leaders should focus on new forms of monetary and non-monetary value exchange.

A Window of Opportunity to Pursue Bold Change

As the world grapples with the effects of a pandemic and the recession it launched us in, every organization is facing a business extinction event: one of those moments when anyone can see that change is imminent, profound, and, for many, catastrophic. In a winner-takes-all market, those who drive change effectively take not only market share but also a greater percentage of profits. Digital Darwinism is unkind to those who wait.

And yet, when it comes to pulling the trigger on taking on the kind of full-out change required to compete in this new world, indecision abounds. Those companies who embraced digital transformation early and failed have realized that scaling and automating a crappy business model that's inappropriate for the market only makes things exponentially worse! As they contemplate taking on another massive change, they are afraid to repeat the same mistakes. And those companies who succeeded in their digital transformation efforts often don't understand where and how to apply the lessons they learned to this next, daunting phase. Faced with this reality and armed with limited data, boards often take too much time to ponder how to proceed next—and then fail to act fast enough.

As nontraditional competitors emerge faster than ever—and as they and existing companies already well on their way to taking the lion's share of a market become bigger and more powerful while their smaller competitors become casualties of the coronavirus economic shutdown—CEOs and their boards are being pressured to reinvent their companies in bold ways despite shareholders' resistance to investing in the long-term at the expense of short-term profit. And it's working. According to a digital transformation study conducted by Constellation in May of 2020, company boards list digital transformation as one of their top three priorities.[7]

The bad news? Digital transformation is only the beginning, the first battle in the upcoming war of building, defending, and battling duopolies. Companies need to move beyond run-of-the-mill digital transformation and engage in a much deeper change if they are to thrive in the age of duopolies. In the next part of the book, I'll show you what that looks like. But for now, the good news is that boards, CEOs, and leaders finally have a window of opportunity to turn the tide amidst the current recovery. Here's why.

Changes to the U.S. tax code together with post-pandemic stimulus packages continue to open up new opportunities for investing capital on long-term projects. The Trump administration's emphasis on reforming trade agreements, as well as the Tax Cuts and Jobs Act (TCJA)—which removed the tax paid by companies on income earned abroad—will result in the collapse of tax havens and less investment outside of the U.S.[8] Constellation estimates that between $353 billion and $417 billion of overseas cash will be repatriated to the United States in the next five years thanks to a one-time tax reduction on income earned abroad before TCJA was enacted. With overseas revenue no longer taxed by the U.S. government, we expect more organizations' headquarters to remain in or move to the U.S. as tax conditions have improved.

Meanwhile, the stimulus packages that the U.S. has extended to business in the wake of the coronavirus economic shutdown will exceed $3 trillion. This influx of cash, thanks to the TCJA and post-pandemic stimulus, will allow companies to invest in long-term innovation and allow them to acquire companies to expand their technical capabilities and the talent pool necessary to pull off a massive transformation.

At the same time, the cost of capital, which is effectively at zero, is leading investors to make investments in growth. The cost of capital for U.S. corporations has dropped from 16.4 percent in 1980 to 5.3 percent in 2015 to essentially nothing now. In fact, the short-term interest rate for savings deposits in Japan is negative 0.1 percent and the rate for long-term ten-year deposits is 0 percent. Any company that wants capital to invest in new product development or equipment or acquisitions necessary to enter a new market, can find it. Organizations that can make the case for either aiming to become a duopoly or present a challenge to one will find easy access to financing.

That has been the case for Reliance Jio, which was founded in 2007 by Mukesh Ambani, one of the wealthiest men alive (net worth $58 billion) and quickly became the fastest growing telecom company in the world. Jio is known for democratizing access to mobile and internet services for hundreds of millions of Indians. As a data-driven digital network, Jio can expand its business and monetization models to its almost 400 million customers well beyond its telecom offerings. They are poised to offer content, network, and tech as well.

Consequently, in 2020, the company raised over $20 billion in financing from outside organizations by selling almost 22 percent of the company to strategic partners such as Abu Dhabi Investment Authority, Facebook, General Atlantic, Google, KKR, Mubadala, Silver Lake, TPG, and Vista Equity Partners. In June of 2020, TPG took a $600 million stake for 0.93 percent of the company, valuing the company at $645 billion. U.S. PE firm L Catterton took a 0.39 percent stake for $250 million in Jio Platforms as the ninth investor in Jio Platforms.[9]

With investors willing to bet on growth, with value chains collapsing, and investments prioritized for resiliency, CEOs and their boards have a unique opportunity to take on the massive task of becoming a viable contender in the age of duopolies—but success won't be easy.

4

INSIDE THE BUSINESS AND MONETIZATION MODELS THAT POWER DATA GIANTS

In late 1999, Toys "R" Us's online business was booming. There was only one problem: They were getting so many orders in anticipation of the holidays, that they couldn't keep up with them. Customers waited weeks to get their purchases, and many didn't receive them until after Christmas. It was a complete debacle, resulting in Toys "R" Us getting fined by the Federal Trade Commission for misrepresenting when they would be able to deliver packages.[1] The next year, to avoid falling into the same problem, Toys "R" Us made a decision, one that eventually would prove fatal: it partnered with Amazon, which agreed to sell its toys and baby products exclusively. The deal was seen as a coup. Amazon, which only two years earlier had gone public, was already the leading e-commerce site.

At first, the Toys "R" Us partnership was a blockbuster, although it came at a high cost.[2] The contract required ToysRus.com to direct all customers to the Amazon site. If someone clicked on an item at ToysRus.com, they were redirected to the Amazon branded site. The toy retailer gave up having its own online retail presence and lost years of experience developing and running its own e-commerce site. For the privilege, it paid Amazon $50 million a year and a couple percentage points for sales through the Amazon site.

In less than four years, however, Amazon failed to maintain exclusivity. Other third-party merchants were also selling toys and baby products and Amazon was either not policing them enough— or may have deliberately allowed these sales to test market reaction. Fed up, Toys "R" Us sued Amazon in May of 2004, eventually winning and receiving more than $50 million in damages.[3]

But the loss was not a big deal for Amazon. Simply by handling Toys "R" Us's online sales, Amazon had learned an enormous amount about the toy and baby category—from what product categories were top sellers to which regions purchased what categories, to which offerings had good margins—at Toys "R" Us's expense. In fact, by the end of their partnership, Amazon had better data about Toys "R" Us's own business than Toys "R" Us did itself.[4] After ending their partnership, the toy retailer was never able to get its e-commerce strategy up to speed, eventually closing all stores after seventy years in business.

Amazon had used Toys "R" Us's own data to compete with it in the digital world. In fact, many well-heeled, highbrow organizations also faced similar experiences. As they watched Amazon's e-commerce lead grow, they flocked to partner with it. It wasn't long before they realized that the power of digital business models rests in the network and the data it collects—and that by partnering with Amazon they were handing their secret recipe (their knowledge of their retail categories and their customer data) to their biggest competitor. Circuit City ended its four-year partnership with Amazon in February of 2005. Borders ended a seven-year agreement in May of 2008. Nike ended an agreement with Amazon to sell its shoes in August 2019.

By learning from these partnerships and other tactics, Amazon dominated the e-commerce market, leading today with a 38.7 percent market share. The nearest nine competitors' combined market share is barely half as large as Amazon's: Walmart (5.3 percent), eBay (4.7 percent), Apple (3.7 percent), Home Depot (1.7 percent), Wayfair (1.5 percent), Best Buy (1.3 percent), Target (1.2 percent), Costco (1.2 percent), Macy's (1.1 percent). Since then, Amazon has used its massive business power in e-commerce to monetize other markets, including streaming video, last mile shipping and logistics, cloud computing, banking, media, and even digital advertising.

If Amazon's partners learned anything it's that one cannot entrust your business model to someone else—you never know if they are just angling to become your competitor.

Build Your Own DDDN

This lesson is one that market leaders live by: They do not trust anyone with their core business model. They know that a seemingly innocent partner who handles a part of their business can and will use their data against them once that partner learns their insights and process tricks—and builds that into a competing business model powered by artificial intelligence. Instead, market leaders map the entire value chain and understand what are the critical points they must control. Their data-driven digital network is one of those critical points of control.

If you want to become a player in the age of duopolies, you must build a data-driven digital network. This DDDN is the heart of every digital giant's business and monetization models. We often talk about business models and monetization models in the same way, but they are, in fact, different. A business model describes how a company generates value for its stakeholders, primarily customers but also suppliers and partners. When developing a business model, you must ask who are your key customers—the market segments—you are targeting. You also have to figure out what value or benefit you will offer customers and your most important stakeholders, and how you will deliver this value. The most common components of business models include: the value proposition, customer segments, customer relationships, key activities, resources, channels, partners, cost structure, and revenue streams.

A monetization model, meanwhile, is part of the business model. It describes how a company generates revenue or income—the financial aspect of "value" generated from customers. But while business models and monetization models are technically two different business concepts, in the industrial age, they were closely connected and "matched." Every business stuck to their lane. For example, Visa competed with Mastercard for charge card dominance. Budweiser battled Miller for beer sales. GM and Ford competed for personal cars and trucks.

However, unique with digital businesses, many companies can share similar business models, which we've described as the same basic way to design, create, capture, and deliver value. But they may pursue very different ways to monetize that value. Or even more interestingly, they may have very different business models but the same monetization model. For example: Google and Facebook both sell digital ads to make money, with Google capturing $75.6 billion (38.2 percent) and Facebook $28.3 billion (21.8 percent) of the total $129.8 billion ad spend in North America. Their nearest competitor is Amazon with $10 billion (6.8 percent) in ad spend. While all three players have adopted the same monetization model (selling ads), they operate very different business models—and each holds a near monopoly within its own business model. Google has decisively won the battle for search; Facebook dominates in social networks; and Amazon has crushed all competition in e-commerce. All three use their respective dominance to fiercely compete for the same pool of ad dollars.

In the Asia-Pacific region, Alibaba, Baidu, and Tencent use the same monetization model of selling advertising, with Alibaba capturing 35.2 percent market share, Baidu 15.4 percent, and Tencent holding on to 12.7 percent of market share. Like their counterparts in the U.S., these three players might share the same monetization model but compete from different positions of strength. Alibaba dominates e-commerce; Baidu is the largest search engine; and Tencent leads in gaming.

Each of these giants in the North American and Asian Pacific regions dominated competitors with the same core business model first, before they expanded to compete with additional business and monetization models. The Chinese internet company Tencent, for example, started out in online gaming. After making money from a subscription model, it built a social network (WeChat) for its gamers from which it was able to generate revenue from advertising as well as from enabling the transaction of digital goods and peer-to-peer payments (where it collects a fee). Tencent didn't stop there. It also entered the entertainment business, producing its own movies and streaming video platform which generates revenue via ads and through product placement. In essence, Tencent built a hundred-year platform, a massive DDDN powered by business and monetization models that keep building on themselves in an organic way, guaranteeing that the DDDN will be around for a long time.

The ability of digital giants to leverage their DDDNs to monetize new markets has allowed them to reach into every industry, value chain, and market, in the process scrambling the traditional lanes between sectors. Given an opportunity, they will expand their business models to spread across as many lanes as they like.

Four Elements of the DDDN Business Model

At the core of the business models that power these digital giants are data-driven digital networks. To build a DDDN business model, you must take into account these four key elements:

1. **A massive user base.** Digital giants pair their company's offering—product, service, or experience—with the largest membership models or groups of users. Cultivating a massive user base is not easy. To create a DDDN, you might need to partner or acquire another company to access the greatest number of users and create a strong network—the user group and a place to create user interactions such as buying and selling, sharing and commenting on content, providing feedback and recommendations, and more. When possible, your DDDN should bring as many networks or groups of users together as possible (such as a network of buyers and a network of sellers) to create multi-sided networks. Airbnb, for example, is a multi-sided network that bring "sellers" or hosts (home and property owners) with "buyers" (renters), matching them with travel services (connecting host and renters to facilitate a short-term rental).

2. **Exponential technologies.** DDDNs rely on new technologies that exponentially differentiate how the company produces or delivers its product, service, or experience—and that creates massive value. Cloud computing enables anywhere access to the internet. Augmented reality and mixed reality enable the creation of new experiences. Blockchain reframes the discussion on networks and trust. Artificial intelligence and automation allow decision-making at a massive scale. Quantum computing changes how problems are solved.

3. **Signal intelligence.** DDDNs leverage user-generated data to fuel the company's competitive advantage. The user (or more accurately, the data the user produces) becomes the product or offering. The value in the data comes from the user interactions (with each other, with products, with the company), which provides "signal intelligence"—critical information

such as what products are trending, which features are not being used, why sales in one county are down, and so on. The company can use the data to make their offerings better, their processes smoother, and their decisions smarter. The result is *digital feedback loops*: Signal intelligence is used to improve offerings, services, or experiences, which in turn attracts more users, which generates even more data, which provides more signal intelligence. That signal intelligence can be learned over time, powered by machine learning. What these DDDNs achieve is a system that improves with more user interactions, data, and knowledge, creating a flywheel effect—a strong competitive barrier to entry and significant advantage over any competitor. This creates a powerful business graph.

4. **A long-term mindset.** DDDNs take a long-view, winner-takes-all approach to lock up the total addressable market by all legal means necessary, backed by investors willing to fund on a ten-year horizon instead of a five-year one.

Now, you would think that you can assemble a DDDN business model by piecing some of these elements in an ad hoc approach. Maybe your business model leverages signal intelligence, but doesn't take the long view. Unfortunately, to create a DDDN business model that will win in the age of duopolies, you must have all four elements at the same time. The synergies of these four elements are what make the DDDN a platform that is powerful and hard to beat. You can't piece just a couple of these elements together. You can't miss any of them.

That is the case with Adobe. In 2011, the creative software giant purchased EchoSign for $400 million, at the time a leading Web-based provider of electronic signatures and signature automation.[5] Over three million users worldwide used the EchoSign Service, which made the process of sending, tracking, and signing digital documents more efficient.[6] Fast forward a decade, and more than 8 billion electronic signatures and digital signature transactions were processed by Adobe Sign, formerly Echo-Sign, in 2019.[7]

While the total market for digital signatures is estimated to cross $6 billion in 2026, the e-commerce software market is exponentially larger with *$7.4 trillion* estimated by 2026. One of the biggest challenges in e-commerce is establishing identity. Sellers want to know who's on the other side of a transaction and if they can trust them. Identity is the heart of all commerce. Identity enables trust. And trust is the most important component of the digital economy. Once your identity is established, you can transact *anonymously* and trusted or *verified* and trusted.

Experts have long advised Adobe to consider how to bring its portfolio from creative software—where it dominates the market for digital tools for creative professionals with products such as Photoshop, Lightroom, InDesign, and Acrobat—to commerce.[8] To do that, in September 2009, CEO Shantanu Narayen started the journey to build out the Adobe Experience, combining advertising, analytics, and marketing into a single platform that would allow companies to take their data and create rich customer profiles they can use to deliver targeted experiences. Adobe sought to build it out this platform through nine significant acquisitions:

- January 23, 2019: Adobe acquires Allegorithmic.[9]
- October 31, 2018: Adobe acquires Marketo.[10]
- June 19, 2018: Adobe acquires Magento Commerce.[11]
- November 10, 2016: Adobe acquires TubeMogul.[12]
- December 11, 2014: Adobe acquires Fotolia.[13]
- June 27, 2013: Adobe acquires Neolane.[14]
- January 16, 2012: Adobe acquires Efficient Frontier.[15]
- October 29, 2010: Adobe acquires Day Software.[16]
- October 23, 2009: Adobe acquires Omniture, Inc.[17]

But despite substantial growth in the market, the Adobe Experience platform has not seen the 40 to 50 percent growth one would expect from these acquisitions. Instead, growth has remained below 30 percent as competitors such as Microsoft, Salesforce.com, and SAP have been competing for the same customers.

However, Adobe has a significant asset that it could leverage to create a DDDN business model that would result in it becoming a digital giant in e-commerce: a massive user base of PDF users. Adobe has 400 million active Adobe PDF users who have created more than 2.5 trillion PDFs. The potential 400 million Adobe PDF users are a bigger network than Twitter (330 monthly active users) and slightly smaller than LinkedIn (575 million monthly active users). Imagine if every PDF user got a validated Adobe Sign account. Adobe would then have an active user base that can transact on commerce, enable payments, and deliver on identity that is almost twice as big as Amazon Prime (140 million) in terms of number of monthly active users.

Adobe could use blockchain technology, a highly secure decentralized digital database, to ensure security and anonymity as needed for each validated transaction. Adobe would ensure that each digital signature would serve as an anonymous but trusted key. Adobe would be able to collect an immense amount of data going forward—type of documents created, the location, devices used, transaction types, and other factors that would be tracked over time creating signal intelligence that could be used to improve not only ease of use of the product, but also to mitigate fraud and improve security. Adobe would be at the center of every trusted transaction and collect a small sliver of $7.4 trillion along the way.

What Adobe has with PDF and Adobe Sign is an opportunity to create a hundred-year platform and become a digital giant poised to rule in the age of duopolies, leaving its competitor DocuSign in the dust. However, Adobe's management team needs to apply a long-term mindset to invest in resources to make this happen. It is sitting on a gold mine but is cautious about investing all of its top people to work on this DDDN asset. Most large organizations can manage three to five different business units at a time. Document Cloud, the unit that manages Adobe Sign product, is one of Adobe's three business units and the smallest. As it is in all large companies that manage a portfolio of businesses, the best team members most likely work on the top products. At Adobe, that would be Creative Cloud, followed by Experience Cloud, then Adobe Document Cloud. Many internal experts at Adobe never expected the Document Cloud team to have as much success as it has and remain so highly profitable with minimal investment. In 2012, many expected Adobe's PDF business to die like Adobe Flash did in 2020. They underinvested and underestimated how fundamental Adobe PDF was to their customers' business workflows.

Adobe has started to put its best people on this game-changing opportunity, instead of exiting or selling it off to someone who can apply the long-term focus and investment needed to build a successful DDDN and create the next digital giant. If Adobe makes the big bets and takes the risks a digital giant would take, it will show how existing players can emerge into a digital giant. Like Adobe, you can have a massive user base, an enabling technology, and signal intelligence—but if you don't take the long-term investment approach and have the risk appetite, you may miss an opportunity to emerge as a digital giant. As this example shows, you need *all four* elements to build a DDDN business model capable of competing in the age of duopolies.

Five Monetization Strategies for DDDNs

Now that we have learned the elements of DDDN business models, let's explore their revenue streams. We often think of companies as having one business model and one monetization model. For example, the public perception is that Amazon just sells goods online. However, digital giants often start with one monetization model and perfect it before expanding to a new one.

There are five ways DDDNs generate revenue: advertising, digital services, digital goods, subscriptions, and memberships. Let's take a deeper look at each of them and how a digital giant, Amazon, has adopted these monetization models over decades, cross-selling and upselling its massive user base.

ADVERTISING

One of the most common monetization models of DDDNs is advertising. When you have access to thousands if not millions (or billions) of users in your network, data about who they are and their preferences is a valuable asset. Using that data to sell advertising that targets your massive user base is a no-brainer. There are six main types of digital ads: display, email marketing, native, social, search, and video.

Display ads are the banners and logos that pop up or are placed on websites. They share text, images, video, and audio to deliver brand messages and advertisements. Social media ads target audiences on platforms such as Facebook, Instagram, Twitter, LinkedIn, and Pinterest with paid ads. The ads emerge in a person's feed based on their search history or what others in that person's social media network may have responded to. Search advertising uses a person's search results to identify and provide the most contextually relevant ads to target that person with. Video advertising takes the form of "in-stream ads" that run before, after, or in the middle of video content, or of "out-stream" ads, video ads placed in banners, for example, that users have to click on to play them. Email marketing is the digital equivalent of a direct mail campaign but done electronically. Native advertising is the paid placement of content that looks and feels like the media format in which it appears (for example, a "paid article" promoting the benefits of a new beauty product, appearing on a lifestyle or health media site).

Companies with DDDN business models gravitate to advertising monetization strategies precisely because their massive data troves allow them to sell highly targeted, contextually relevant product messages. Their ad services, powered by machine learning technology, zero in on commonly searched terms to suggest and optimize product recommendations. For instance, if the service detects a lot of searches for the color purple, ads will shift to show more purple-colored goods, users will be served up relevant reviews of purple products, and only users that search for the purple color will be solicitated for online survey feedback. These ad services also use the information they collect to predict relevant ads. For example, a user clicks a lot of ads for toilet paper, hair dye, hand sanitizer, PPE supplies, and disinfectant wipe in the spring of 2020. A smart ad service would figure out that a few months later, those ads would no longer be effective unless a new pandemic leads to more stay-at-home orders. The service, instead, would start targeting that user with ads for bikes or RVs or products and services to help that user move out of the city.

The digital advertising market is over $100 billion worldwide. Google dominates with over 37 percent of the market while Facebook comprises 22 percent of the U.S. digital ad spend. Amazon has grown to 8.8 percent of ad spend, while Microsoft and LinkedIn have about 3.8 percent of the market and Verizon Media has 2.9 percent. By all accounts, Google and Facebook won the first battle. However, Amazon is growing both revenue and market share at a massive clip. With over 112 million prime members and 310 million accounts, Amazon is using its power as the reigning duopoly in commerce to make a play for the ad market dominated by the Google and Facebook duopolies. It started in 2008, when Liza Utzschneider came from Microsoft to build the advertising business. Amazon mostly started selling display and search ads for its commerce platform. However, with the launch of Prime Video, Amazon has also entered the market for product placements in their own movie and TV productions and email marketing campaigns advertising other studios' offerings. The sophistication of Amazon's advertising offerings has increased, as they have expanded to coupons, recurring orders, space on shipping boxes, embedded buttons, and even their own ad networks on other websites. Amazon has also experimented with allowing brands who don't sell on Amazon to advertise. Today, Amazon is monetizing almost $10 billion in ad sales along with the rest of its properties.

In September of 2019, Amazon brought all its ad properties together under one roof. Now Amazon Media Group, Amazon Advertising Platform, and Amazon Marketing Services are known as Amazon Advertising, under the control of Amazon's ad boss Paul Kotas. The full power of their DDDN comes together as Amazon Advertising is able to pull data from all of Amazon's commerce interactions. This allows them to tie ads to purchases back to marketing campaigns and back. They now have complete end-to-end ownership of the customer journey data: from the time a customer searches for a product, to the product being delivered, to the customer survey being deployed on the back end, and to the purchases customers make next. Brands and sellers have sought this holy grail of closed-loop targeting without having to worry about privacy issues. In Amazon's case, the data is all in one closed network. Amazon is no longer just a sellers' market, it is also an advertising platform, and a supply chain signal on demand.

DIGITAL SERVICES

Another common revenue stream for data giants is selling digital services—the electronic delivery of data, content, processes, or insight. These services give customers or user access but no title or ownership. For example, the digital service might be the ability to use or access software or a library of content, like streaming videos. If you were to sell ownership to the software or a video, that would make it a digital good. These services depend on information technology resources as they are delivered via the internet, often requiring very little human interaction.

In many cases, digital services are delivered for free as part of a "freemium to premium" campaign or in order to improve adoption and drive data collection to power the DDDN. When the service is free, the individual and their data become the "payment." The value exchange for a "free" service, in other words, is the ability to monetize the user's data—such as location data, the user's search results, and their interactions with other users—to sell them ads or make recommendations.

Amazon's Web Services is a good example of a purely digital service. It provides brands and enterprises the cloud computing power they need to power their e-commerce sites: digital storage for emails, videos, chats, social media, and business data; and computing power to crunch transactions, tell you the weather, help you upload a social media file, or access your map on your phone. Amazon originally built its cloud mainly to support its commerce, especially during peak times. To support their operations and handle the sheer number of transactions processed on busy times such as Mother's Day, Prime Day, Cyber Monday, and the holidays, Amazon must build excess capacity. Today, anyone wanting to build a mobile app, launch a site, or get deep on AI can pay to use Amazon's cloud, even its competitors. However, any potential competitors with a similar business or monetization model who uses

Amazon are, essentially, subsidizing Amazon's ability to crush them in commerce and other business models. With Amazon Web Services, Amazon has effectively turned their excess capacity from a cost liability to a profitable asset that brings in more than half of Amazon's revenues, around $300 billion a year, and captures a 33.4 percent market share (with 33.2 percent growth). Its nearest competitor is not one to laugh at: Microsoft Azure holds a 14.9 percent market share and is growing at 62.3 percent year over year, while Google Cloud has a 4.9 percent market share and is growing at 67 percent.

This is not the only digital service-based monetization strategy in Amazon's arsenal. Amazon has also mastered streaming services. Amazon's streaming service, which competes with Netflix, known as Amazon Prime Video, enables users to receive all digital media: From the first CD you bought in 1999 to the latest movie you purchased, Amazon allows you to access the entire collection in the cloud for $8.99 per month. While new competitors from AppleTV+ to HBO Max to Comcast's Peacock are coming into the mix, Amazon has the computing power, the content from their library, and a massive network of 112 million Amazon Prime members in the U.S.

DIGITAL GOODS

Another monetization model that DDDNs adopt is selling digital goods. Unlike selling digital services which only grant users access to digital content, selling a digital good grants customers perpetual use of it—they get to keep it forever. Common examples of digital goods include software, music, movie or TV downloads, photos, eBooks, coupons, virtual goods (non-physical assets sold in virtual economies like online games), electronic live event tickets, apps, and avatars. Some digital goods are representations of physical goods. For example, an eBook is a digital version of the physical book. A piece of artwork that is "to-kenized" means that a verifiable representation of the art is stored in a blockchain as a digital twin.

A successful digital goods strategy creates massive scale for DDDNs. You can develop a product once and deliver the same exact good to millions or billions of customers through the internet. It is a low-cost approach to taking a product from concept to commercialization. Since digital goods have zero marginal costs, this strategy has a significant advantage over selling physical goods. However, digital goods are often rigid, meaning once delivered, they cannot be easily modified, changed, or altered.

Amazon's digital goods strategy includes selling software, music, games and apps, eBooks via Kindle, and audiobooks via Audible. Audible, for example, has sold 725 million downloaded audios to its subscribers.[18]

SUBSCRIPTIONS

Subscription models—when users or customers pay a set fee in regular intervals in exchange for access to a product, service, or experience—have been a common monetization strategy for digital giants. These models typically provide users different levels of access at various price points. For example, in a freemium model, a game like Angry Birds is free to use up to the tenth level. After that, you must pay a subscription to gain access to the game. The advantage of subscription models is that they enable users to get access to goods or services on their own terms. As Tien Tzuo, author of *Subscribed*, and legendary CEO of Zuora explains, "Customers are happier subscribing to the outcomes they want, when they want them, rather than purchasing a product with the burden of ownership."[19]

Because companies have to earn the customer's business again at the end of each renewal period, subscription models also force companies to improve their responsiveness to users' needs and requests. At the same time, companies benefit from the predictability of recurring revenue by managing retention and customer satisfaction.

Amazon has worked a subscription monetization strategy into its business model by allowing customers the chance to "subscribe" to certain products—for example, diapers and baby wipes, or beauty products like lotions and shampoos, or cleaning supplies like laundry detergent—which are then delivered automatically at a specific interval (typically every few weeks). In exchange for subscribing, customers get a discount off the listed price. Customers can even subscribe to services, such as their home protection "Ring Protect Plan" video doorbell subscription or to curated product boxes. One of the popular services is the STEM club, which allows parents of kids age eight to thirteen to subscribe to science, technology, engineering, and math toys and resources. Similarly, Prime Book Box delivers new age-appropriate children's books to customers on a regular basis. Customers can manage these subscriptions—and third party ones such as magazine subscriptions—on the Subscribe with Amazon page on their website. Subscribe with Amazon provides the digital giant with an easy recurring revenue stream, and gives it two significant competitive advantages. One, the money stays within Amazon as customers commit to spending their dollars on their site. Two, this level of account control effectively locks out existing and future competitors.

MEMBERSHIPS

Membership monetization models go beyond subscriptions. While both membership and subscription models offer access to products, services, or experiences in exchange for a fee that is paid at regular intervals, the membership model also includes a community where users get to connect, share ideas and recommendations, and many other non-financial benefits. Memberships gives users a sense of belonging, a shared purpose, and an opportunity to connect with like-minded people. In some cases, members pay dues to save money, access common services, or attend events.

Costco.com is a great example of a mission-driven company that has mastered the membership monetization model and that could evolve into a digital giant. Costco members know that they are going to get high quality and value with each shopping experience. This allows Costco to expand its offerings from hot water heater installation, to auto buying, to business delivery and payment processing. All they need is a community of fans and a commerce network and Costco.com could be on its way to dominate the home services market from HVAC to solar panel installation.

With Amazon Prime, Amazon has bundled subscription services into a membership model. Most members join Prime to benefit from year-round free next-day or same-day shipping, discounts at Whole Foods and 5 percent cash back on the Amazon Prime Rewards Visa Card. But for an annual fee of $119, Amazon Prime also provides users with a subscription to a bundle of services: Prime Video, ad-free music streaming, unlimited photo storage, and unlimited reading. The membership model unifies the brand and creates a higher degree of cross-sell and upsell revenue. The result is lower customer acquisition costs and higher revenue per user, which is what DDDNs are measured on.

Every DDDN must find a way to monetize the five monetization models: advertising, digital goods, digital services, subscriptions, and memberships. Some DDDNs will focus on one, but eventually the leaders will apply multiple digital monetization models as they compete for the highest profit per customer.

From Miles to Cryptocurrencies: A Tale of Two Mileage Programs

Throughout this chapter, I've shown that to dance with digital giants, you'll first need to build a compelling DDDN business and monetization model. Doing so is not without challenges, even when you have most of the elements to pull it off. The story of two airline frequent flyer miles programs illustrates precisely that.

Airlines had some of their best years ever from 2010 to 2019, generating over $250 billion in total profits. Coming back from the 2008 recession, they beat all key performance indicators: $247.6 billion in revenues in 2019, a backlog of Airbus (7482) and Boeing (5625) jet orders, and an all-time travel record with 4.723 billion passengers.[20] The airlines and their partners were riding high on success. But as revenues per mile or kilometers were growing, few airlines chose to innovate one of their biggest assets: their loyalty programs.

Frequent flyer programs for all airlines are estimated to generate as much as $10 billion in revenues with over 40 percent in margins. Flyers earn frequent flyer miles and accumulate them like dollars in a bank: The miles might not earn interest, but they mostly don't expire and can be redeemed through the airline and its partners. As airlines seek new monetization models, frequent flyer miles programs could emerge as de facto fiat currency: cross-border, universally accepted, non-taxable, and ubiquitous.

A mileage program that used blockchain to create a travel crypto currency and digital wallet is not such a crazy idea. Large airline networks such as the Star Alliance—the international network of airlines formed by Scandinavian Airlines, Thai Airways International, Air Canada, Lufthansa, and United Airlines—serve more than 762 million members.[21] Sky Team has 630 million members.[22] Oneworld has 528 million members.[23] If any of these global alliances would create a crypto currency, it would emerge as a fiat currency overnight with over 500 million users on day one.

Back in 2018, one frequent flyer program had a unique opportunity to emerge as a cryptocurrency. The Aeroplan program was created in 1984 as Air Canada's loyalty program for its frequent flyers. After being spun off as a separate corporate entity and eventually sold off, Air Canada, along with three banks—Toronto Dominion, CIBC, and Visa—acquired it back again in 2018 for CA $450 million in cash.

Aeroplan, a member of the Star Alliance, has over 5 million members who earn and redeem miles through flights, and also through its many partners. These include Avis Budget Group and major hotel chains like Starwood Hotels & Resorts and Fairmont Hotels & Resorts. Aeroplan also has extensive partnerships with credit card companies such as American Express Canada, and their owners Toronto Dominion Bank and CIBC. [24] Finally, their retail partners include Birks, Home Hardware, and Nestle Canada, and the more than 170 flagship retail brands featured in eStore, Aeroplan's online shopping portal.[25] In 2019, over 2.8 million rewards were redeemed, including 2.1 million flights. Since launching non-air rewards in 2004, more than 190 billion Aeroplan miles have been redeemed for merchandise, car rentals, hotel stays, and other experiential rewards.[26]

All the conditions to successfully build a digital giant were in place. Aeroplan had a massive group of users. The loyalty program had large data sets connected to networks (their travel, banking, and retail partners). Airline global distribution systems (GDS) have a lot of demographic and interaction history information that can be used to improve personalization and optimize pricing. And a then new technology, blockchain, could enable a cryptocurrency. Everything was right in front of them to turn their program into a hundred-year platform or DDDN.

So why didn't Aeroplan do it?

Once again, corporate culture played a significant role in halting its chances to create a new business model. Aeroplan chose to focus on stability and avoid taking major risks. The lack of a long-term mindset meant that Aeroplan was not interested in expanding into new markets but more focused on making quarter-to-quarter expectations. The result was a return to the old stodgy frequent flyer program and little innovation to the successor product.

Meanwhile, on the other side of the world, another airline began an initiative to radically change the business model for its frequent flyer program. On February 2018, Singapore Airlines launched the world's first blockchain-based airline loyalty digital mileage wallet. Named KrisPay, its tagline is "mobile miles for every day spend." [27] Under this program, customers can convert their Singapore Airlines KrisFlyer air miles into KrisPay miles that can be spent on non-travel related products from their partner brands.

Singapore Airlines did what Aeroplan wouldn't: It evolved from a loyalty program to a value exchange system, in essence a new fiat currency. Rachel Tan, product lead at KrisPay stated, "We heard from our customers that they wanted more redemption options, relevant to their everyday spending, so their miles do not go to waste. This inspired our team to develop KrisPay, the world's first blockchain-based airline loyalty digital miles wallet, which enables our customers to pay with their miles instantly for purchases at partner outlets, right from their mobile phones." [28]

Customers earn miles when traveling via flights, hotel partners, and transport partners. They can also earn miles when they dine at select restaurant partners from donut shops to bubble tea shops. Over 2,000 online retail partners are part of the KrisPay network. Credit card partners also give customers the ability to earn miles. Customers can then use these miles to pay for everything from shoes to candy to gas to meals at a huge number of restaurants. In addition, KrisPay provides personalized offers based on customers' declared interests and location-based data. As customers indicate more preferences and share more data, KrisPay provides higher levels of personalized services.

In an interview with *CIO*, Siak Chuah Tan, technology lead in Information Technology at KrisPay, explained that blockchain technology was key to the program's success. Singapore Airlines took six months to create the program using Azure Blockchain Service. Overnight KrisPay has become a symbol of digital trust and commerce on a member network.

Building a cryptocurrency masked as a frequent flyer program brings many benefits not only to the issuer, in this case Singapore Airlines, but also to the customer:

1. **Eases of use value exchange.** Cryptocurrency-based frequent flyer programs or loyalty systems provide customers a wider range of redemption options that are not tied to travel, blackout dates, or limited unfunded availability (the industry term for seats not available because there are no reward travel seats).

2. **Improves loyalty.** Members recognize the advantage of being part of a greater network of partners, encouraging them to continue spending on the network.

3. **Minimizes depreciation.** The exchange rate mechanism for redemption creates a market value for the tokens or point system, instead of the steady depreciation of mile redemption that normally occurs in regular frequent flyer programs.

4. **Increases perishable inventory and drives up margin.** In 2018, Singapore Airlines spent more than $700 million in

deferred revenue waiting for outstanding miles to be redeemed on seats.[29] Encouraging members to redeem for other goods besides a free seat increases profits while reducing risk.

5. **Creates a new fiat currency.** An initial coin offering (ICO) would allow Singapore Airlines an opportunity to raise capital by selling miles, issuing stock, or creating more value. This money could be used to reinvest or raise revenue for investment. In addition, Singapore Airlines could take 25,000 miles cashed in by a customer to sell those miles in a market for cash on redemption.

As the first mover in place, Singapore Airlines has opened the eyes of its competitors and of companies in other markets to the possibilities in front of them. Lufthansa and Air New Zealand have already partnered with Winding Tree, a Swiss-based startup, to develop blockchain-based travel apps. Cathay Pacific's frequent flyer program, Asia Miles, is trying to create their digital wallet with a dining program. Sandblock (SAT) seeks to bring small businesses and their loyalty programs together in a larger consortium built on another blockchain standard known as Ethereum.

Even now, when airlines are in a slump due to the COVID-19 pandemic, they still have an opportunity to apply the four elements of DDDN business models to their loyalty programs. Airlines already have massive user base with 2 billion members of loyalty programs. Blockchain can play a key role as the exponential technology. All the travel data they collect from global distribution systems that show passengers, flight plans, customer preferences, destinations, and spend would provide significant signal intelligence. All they need are leaders with a long-term mindset and who see the possibility for a radical new future.

5

PURSUE DECISION VELOCITY

Speed has always been a critical success factor in winning wars on the battlefield. You need to move troops faster, reach targets more quickly, and strike with speed and precision. However, what is often not talked about is how the speed with which *decisions* are made plays a role in claiming victory. Alexander the Great's success on the battlefield is often credited to the rapid decision-making capabilities of his armies. Enabled by trust and a decentralized command structure, his troops were able to beat their enemies by "out-decisioning" them. In most cases, his opponents had bureaucratic decision architectures, where minor decisions would travel up multiple levels of command before traveling back down to be executed. In the 330s BC, that could mean it took days to make a decision on the battlefield. Such a centralized control and detailed micro-management approach was no match for Alexander the Great's nimble teams. British military strategist J. F. C. Fuller, writing on Alexander the Great, explained, "Time was his constant ally; he capitalized every moment, never pondered on it, and thereby achieved his ends before others had settled on their means."[1]

The speed of decision making plays a similar role in the age of digital giants. Any organization that can make decisions twice as fast or one hundred times faster than its competitors will decimate them. Time is a friend to those who make can make faster, more accurate decisions. While the human brain may take minutes to make a decision and it takes hours for a decision to work through an internal organizational structure, in the digital world machines and artificial intelligence engines can make a decision in milliseconds. Whomever masters these automated decisions at high velocity will have an exponential advantage over those who don't.

For your DDDN to become a digital giant and be among the few who rise to a duopoly, they must achieve decision velocity: First you have to amass a huge number of users and collect rich data and insights about their interactions—what I call data supremacy. Then you must train artificial intelligence to recognize patterns in that data and automate decisions, processes, and tasks based on those patterns. The higher the number of users, the higher the number of interactions, the higher the amount of data, the higher the quality of insights that AI can learn from, the higher the level of automation of your decisions in your organization. The higher the level of automation of the organization's decisions, the higher chances you'll rule your market.

It All Starts with Quality Data—Lots of It

Data is the foundation and the first priority for every DDDN's growth and development. You must find and harvest all relevant sources of data and control, if not own, the upstream raw data sources. On the downstream side, you must control access to how the data is shared, monetized, and controlled. This means identifying where the biggest pools of quality data reside and understanding how data is consumed inside the organization.

However, the battle for data is often misunderstood. Many think data supremacy is only about accumulating the greatest troves of data. But having the most data does not necessarily mean you win. This is a battle for the most insight from well-curated, highly contextual data. *Quality* trumps quantity. The real goal is to understand the *relationships* among data. You want to learn how the data interacts with each other and what patterns arise from these interactions.

Where does the raw data come from? Successful DDDNs mine their organizations top to bottom, harvesting data from enterprise transactional systems like their accounting systems, supply chain, operations, and performance data. Then they pair their baseline back office data with front office data that includes customer interactions from sales, marketing, service, and commerce. They also mine "machine-generated data"—log files from equipment—and external sources such as social media feeds and feedback surveys.

The next source of data DDDNs rely on is user-generated. Every DDDN gets excited whenever users provide data on their own, whether through an online resume, a social profile, a customer account for a website, payment information, location data when they "check in" to a restaurant or shop, or photos that can be used for facial recognition and image recognition. The more DDDNs drive engagement with their users, the richer the data sets they collect and the more opportunities they have to find insight in the data.

These insights come from correlations, associations, and relationships—their "interactions"—among all the data produced and captured. Successful DDDNs are masters at identifying "signal intelligence," the meaningful patterns or trends that emerge from the cacophony of data interactions. And they use this signal intelligence to make all sorts of "precision decisions," from how much to charge for a product, to what customers ought to be targeted for what marketing campaign, to what product should be recommended to what customers.

LinkedIn is one such successful DDDN. The premiere social network and community for business professionals is owned by Microsoft and has just over 706 million members across more than 150 countries.[2] You've probably used LinkedIn and know that members create the equivalent of a resume or curriculum vitae (CV) on the platform. They start by creating a profile and inputting key career information such as the start and end dates of their various positions they held over the years. In addition, they provide richer and more descriptive details that summarize their work experiences, education, skillset, activities, and education. LinkedIn also provides a social media publishing platform so members can share their thoughts via short posts, blogs, video, and even live events broadcasting. Once a profile has been completed members reach out to their contacts to connect with them. Members can also search the network and ask to be connected or have someone recommend them to another member.

The value of the LinkedIn network comes from the unique data that emerges from members' interactions with one another and their engagement in the platform. Understanding how people are connected, what interests drive engagement, where people are from, what backgrounds and skills they have, and how often they engage provides "a social graph" that documents the relationships between users and between users and the site's content—and then to identify patterns in them. This social graph has the power to provide signal intelligence about the economy—insights into geography, jobs, skills, educational institutions, companies, demographics—recommendations that help answer key questions such as, "What's the most popular skill required for a job in Silicon Valley?" or "What's the top job and destination for recent college graduates?" Companies, planning agencies, and investors can use these key economic signals to help them plan ahead. For example, recruiters can determine the ten hot skills in demand. Companies can plan ahead for office space requirements in popular locales. They can also use their own performance data on college recruiting to see which schools they should double down on for top skills.

Growing the Data Sources

Since more quality data equals more signal intelligence, DDDNs are always trying to exponentially grow their data sources by adding more networks to it to form what's called a multi-sided network. Classic examples of multi-sided networks are procurement networks like SAP Ariba or a marketplace like eBay. These networks have buyers on one side and sellers on the other. By bringing together these two networks, a DDDN can gather data about demand (who's interested in buying what), as well as data about supply (who's offering a product, service, or experience). Sifting through the data produced by the interaction of these two networks, the DDDN gathers signal intelligence such as determining what's the optimal price a buyer will pay for products from a seller.

That's why social networks, large membership organizations, and big subscriber bases are so important to the success of a DDDN: Harvesting rich data requires having a highly engaged, massive user base that is constantly producing interactions. The richness of these interactions power signal intelligence. Networks of connected devices can also produce rich data and signal intelligence. There are over 31 billion devices such as smart thermostats, smart speakers, industrial sensors, security cameras, and fitness apps connected to the internet. That's more than three times the number of humans—and they are producing their own rich data: where devices are located and how they are interacting with each other, with humans, and with other networks.

When we study how a massive user base interacts with each other or with these billions of devices, we gain insights and identify patterns of behavior known as ontologies. For example, a pattern could emerge that e-commerce customers who read positive reviews of a product (e.g., four or higher stars out of five) prior to shopping tend to spend more on an average than those who do not visit any review sites at all. Another pattern could show customers that purchase in the first hour of a marketing campaign are more likely to come back again. This signal intelligence can be used to personalize the customer experience. The more users, the more data. The more data, the more signal intelligence. The more signal intelligence, the more precision decisions that can be made (such as personalizing a customer experience).

The problem is that the volume of data produced by these multi-sided networks and that powers this critical signal intelligence often exceeds petabytes. How much is a petabyte? Well, a gigabyte is about seven minutes of 4K video. A petabyte is a million gigabytes—or 117,000 hours of 4K video! There is really no way for humans to process this amount of data and signal intelligence to make fast precision decisions. That's why DDDNs that have achieved data supremacy—that have amassed this treasure trove of data and signal intelligence—rely on AI and machine learning to help fine-tune their precision decisions at scale, and achieve decision velocity.

Data Supremacy at a 130-Year-Old Data Giant

A company that has truly achieved data supremacy is Royal Philips, the 130-year-old Netherlands-based multinational conglomerate with over $20 billion in revenues. The company has three divisions: Personal Health (formerly Philips Consumer Electronics and Philips Domestic Appliances and Personal Care), Connected Care, and Diagnosis & Treatment. The shift from electronics and lighting to consumer healthcare makes Royal

Philips one of the largest healthcare technology companies in the world, competing with the likes of Siemens, GE Healthcare, and Canon for duopoly status. The company focuses on improving people's health and enabling better outcomes along a continuum from healthy living and prevention to diagnosis, treatment, and home care. Data plays a crucial role in Royal Philips's long-term strategy of harnessing signal intelligence to improve products, identify health trends, and deliver preventive care services.

In the healthcare provider space, Royal Philips' HealthSuite brings massive amounts of clinical data into one digital platform. With more than 390 million medical images and collected patient information—the equivalent of 21 petabytes of data—the technology provider has a trove of information that can improve decision-making for providers, clinicians, front-line healthcare workers, data scientists, and technologists to improve health outcomes. For example, combining two disparate data points—a chronology of lung images that identifies how long a patient has had a tumor and that patient's prescription medication history—can potentially identify drugs that are increasing the patient's tumor and lung cancer risks. Medical professionals can potentially save a life and insurers can reduce the cost of care by preventing the spread of a tumor. As healthcare providers use insights to improve care, patient data is crucial to delivering precision decisions.

A partnership with Amazon Web Services (AWS) provides the heart of the solution, a regulatory-compliant cloud platform that connects with other DDDNs such as electronic medical records, pharmacy systems, and more. The cloud platform also facilitates the collection, aggregation, storage, and analysis of insights from electronic health data. The platform also brings together key data sources from consumer and enterprise IoT devices to manage, monitor, update, and collect data from smart devices. Patients and users can identify, communicate with, and monitor clinical-grade and consumer health devices such as ear thermometers, blood pressure monitors, body analysis scales, and health watches. Royal Phillips's goal? To improve how easily patients can self-monitor via wearables, smart devices, and other ambient sensing technologies.

In many interviews, Royal Philips has affirmed these goals. "The digital health revolution and the power of the Internet of Things offer tremendous opportunities to positively transform how care is delivered," said Jeroen Tas, CEO of Philips Healthcare Informatics, Solutions and Services. "By unleashing data from connected devices and health records, combined with analytics, valuable insights into how we can live and age well can be uncovered. At Philips, we seek to empower consumers to be active participants in their own health. For example, by giving them access to and control over their own health information, making that data more actionable, and by facilitating better collaboration between patients, clinicians, and caregivers."[3]

Royal Philips understands it is important to expand their network by collaborating with a large ecosystem. The HealthSuite digital platform brings a network built on patient records while the IoT capabilities captures data from devices including medical alert systems and baby monitors. Philips's secure device cloud already manages more than 7 million connected devices, sensors, and mobile apps. The ability to bring more interactions to the network can improve their signal intelligence and leads to faster diagnoses, reduces risk, and improves actionable insight.

The endgame for Royal Phililps is a multisided network of providers, insurance companies, device manufacturers, and patient consumers. This march toward data supremacy is setting Philips up to potentially create one of the winning duopolies built on healthcare data.

Automating Precision Decisions with the Help of AI

To fine-tune precision decisions at scale—that is, to develop decision velocity—DDDNs must automate the process of turning signal intelligence into a decision or action. And the way to do this is by creating AI smart services—automated processes powered by AI. For example, to determine how quickly to pay an invoice, an AI smart service will sift through data available—how much cash on hand the company has, currency exchange rates, customer status, and special contract terms—to make a decision (pay right away, in thirty days, ninety days, and so on).

But AI smart services are not easy to master. They require more than just great algorithms. In order to develop AI smart services to deliver precision decisions at scale and achieve decision velocity, DDDNs must meet these six requirements:

1. **Massive computing power.** To develop AI smart services, DDDNs must have access to or own cheap computing power. The ultimate metric for AI rests in pricing not in terms of computing power, but in terms of potential cost per kilowatt hour. The cheapest rate of computing power may determine the cost structure for AI smart services. The most efficient code for finding signal intelligence will provide a cost advantage for each decision made.

2. **Time**. There is no substitute for time. The algorithms that power AI smart services need lots of training to improve their precision. They need time to understand nuance, exceptions, and context to make better decisions. As the network grows and produces more data and interactions, the AI smart services need more time to identify new patterns. That's why early adopters who train their AI smart services to process the massive petabytes of data coming into them gain an advantage.

The earlier and the quicker the AI smart services learn, the more precision they put back into their algorithms. The ability to compress time, or take tasks that would normally take weeks and complete them in minutes, provides DDDNs an inherent advantage over their competitors.

3. **Awesome math talent.** People enable artificial intelligence; algorithms are only as good as the math talent behind it. Success requires hiring digital artisans—those who can balance right brain and left brain expertise. Digital giants typically have armies of data scientists and a brain trust on hand to fine tune AI smart services for their DDDNs.

4. **Vertical specific expertise.** To make precision decisions, AI smart services must understand nuances of the various verticals in which they operate—e.g., size of company (such as small businesses), industries (like banking), and cultural regions (like Catalonia in Spain). These verticals take time to understand and master. Data supremacy in one vertical can provide a base of understanding to learn another. The more vertical-sophisticated and specialized the AI smart service, the more likely it is to produce precision decisions that are relevant to the end users. As networks from different verticals and membership bases connect with other networks, a "flywheel effect" develops. For example, the intersection of three separate networks in banking, small business, and in Barcelona creates more vertical specific data, which powers more nuanced signal intelligence and becomes self-generating, identifying complex patterns that can help, say, a bank provide microlending to a street food vendor in Barcelona who wants to expand her business.

5. **Natural user interfaces and user experiences.** DDDNs must develop AI smart services that engage users in a variety of

human computer interfaces that mimic human interaction in terms of their sensory, visualization, voice, and gesture capabilities. The interfaces might range from chat bots to virtual assistants, and from augmented reality to brain wave mind readers and computer vision. Users will be able to talk to the system, use gestures and touch to interact with it in augmented and virtual reality, and even have their brain waves control the system. The more blended and natural these experiences become, the more easily these systems will be adopted by users of the DDDN.

6. **Contextually relevant recommendations.** The output of any AI smart services must be a suggestion or recommendation for actions or a choice between several actions. For example, a resort that consumes a hundred rolls of toilet paper per stall might rely on an AI smart service to track how quickly the toilet paper is used and make choice recommendations based on its usage. The system, for example, might recommend that an operator manually reorder more toilet paper, or it can be given automatic approval to make that order based on certain conditions. Each choice has a context, and every decision made by a user, operator, customer, or any stakeholder provides a signal that is observed. Over time, the decisions the users make based on the AI smart service recommendation help improve the precision of its future recommendations. Once users are confident about how the system arrives at a recommendation, these AI-driven smart services start automating decisions—augmenting humanity, accelerating decision making, and ultimately providing filters that deliver situational awareness (the ability to perceive one's surroundings, events in a timeline, and the potential future state).

Understand the Different Outcomes of AI Smart Services

AI smart services can deliver different outcomes—they can automate simple processes like keeping track of inventory, or complex processes such as automatically ordering new stock when the system detects customers have shown special or unusual interest in an item. As you create AI smart services for your DDDN, it's important to understand the seven outcomes that can be achieved with them and how they can enable decision velocity:

1. **Perception.** The AI smart service describes what's happening now. It provides a rudimentary description of the surroundings as manually programmed. For example, a retail system that tells you there are thirty blue pants left in the back room, five in the changing room, two with a cashier, and one with a customer who hasn't left the store.

2. **Notification.** The AI smart service tells you what you asked to know. It provides notifications through alerts, reminders, and other signals that help deliver additional information through manual input and learning. For example, as the retail system improves, a notification may be created to alert staff whenever inventory that is in high demand is left in the changing room. Staff now know to return clothes to the floor so the store doesn't miss the opportunity to sell them. The AI smart service can observe how and when a store clerk reacts to the notification so it can learn what recommended actions to suggest in the future.

3. **Suggestion.** AI smart service recommends action. It offers suggestions for what to do built on past behaviors and modified over time based on weighted attributes, decision management,

and machine learning. Back to the retail example, the system might suggest that staff check the changing area whenever a hot item—e.g., skinny jeans in size 6—is perceived to be in the changing room. Based on the past sales figures for this item, the time of year, the day of the week, and even the shift, the system recommends bringing this item back on the display shelf within twenty minutes or less.

4. **Automation.** AI smart services repeat what you always want. As the system learns over time, it fine-tunes and automates the notifications and suggestions for actions. In the retail case, when only two pairs of a size are on display, staff will automatically get a notification alerting them about how many skinny jeans are in the changing room and suggesting how much time they have to put them out on the display.

5. **Prediction.** AI smart services informs you what to expect. Prediction builds on deep learning to anticipate and test for behaviors. For example, based on over a thousand interactions, the retail store manager will receive a forecast when the store opens for the day that predicts they will be out of skinny jeans in size 6 by 2:00 p.m. The manager will automatically then receive a prompt, asking whether she would like to order more for arrival by midday. If the store manager always says yes, the system will learn to always check stock and suggest the manager order inventory accordingly. After five thousand orders, the store manager may just give the system carte blanche to automatically fulfill inventory.

6. **Prevention.** AI smart services help you avoid bad outcomes. It applies cognitive reckoning, or its accumulated knowledge, to identify potential threats. In the case of a retailer, AI smart services might help to identify potential credit card fraud

before someone makes a purchase. The benefits might be even more powerful in a case where a product or service is being returned for defects. In that case, AI smart services that focus on prevention are all about mitigating risk. For example, on September 2, 2016, Samsung recalled its Galaxy mobile devices due to the potential for their batteries to catch on fire. Retailers scrambled to address the recall. It turns out that during the total period of the recall, a mere 150 phones out of 2.5 million units (which represents 0.006% of the phones produced, a very high sigma in quality) were affected. The recall cost $16 billion over eight weeks.[4] If an AI smart service that optimizes recalls had been in place, Samsung might have been able to trace the defective phones more quickly and save money. Moving to a one week recall might have cost them only $1 billion. A one-day recall may have cost them only $100 million. What's a $1 million investment in AI-powered software to save $100 million or even $16 billion? Decision velocity for preventing bad outcomes always pays for itself.

7. **Situational awareness.** AI smart services tells you what you need to know right now. Situational awareness—knowing what's going in that particular time and place and what to do in that situation—comes close to mimicking human decision-making. Achieving full situational awareness is the most desired outcome of an AI smart service and the one that can deliver the highest level of decision velocity. See Figure 5.1.

When and How to Automate at Scale

If you are building a DDDN to achieve decision velocity, you will likely not have the resources to create AI smart services to intelligently automate *every* process or decision in their organization. You'll need to prioritize. AI is great when you have simple tasks

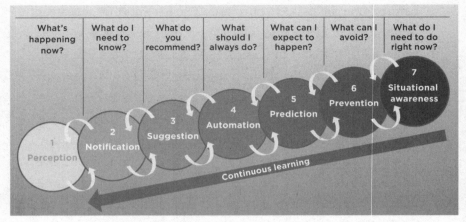

FIGURE 5.1. SPECTRUM OF SEVEN OUTCOMES FOR AI.

that need to be automated to handle volume and to do it fast, and really complex tasks that are beyond human processing abilities. There are seven factors to consider when deciding which processes and decision, when automated, will deliver the greatest payoff (see Figure 5.2):

1. **Repetitiveness.** The greater the frequency with which a process must be repeated, the more likely it should be AI-powered. Highly repeatable processes, especially those in areas well defined by regulations, are perfect candidates. For example, giving customers a chance to opt-in to emails or collecting contact information for marketing purposes are both processes that are well-defined and are required by every customer on an annual basis. Creating AI smart services that identify the right customer accounts that need to be updated and automatically sending requests to opt-in or to provide updated contact information would enable decision velocity.

2. **Volume.** When the volume of transactions and interactions associated with a process or task exceeds human capacity, then this process should be AI-powered. A password reset or an

accounts receivable are examples of high-volume processes that benefit from automation.

3. **Time to complete.** High time-to-market requirements favor AI-powered approaches. Lower time-to-completion requirements will remain human-powered. For example, a company moving from a monthly financial close to a weekly or daily financial close will suddenly need to exponentially increase the speed in which it performs these tasks. Even the best finance departments need a day to manually close on a weekly basis. Since the time-to-completion would exceed the time and resources available at the right budget to perform this task, it is a perfect candidate for automation.

4. **High-volume and complex interactions.** Human-powered efforts fail when a DDDN must interface with billions of users and trillions of engagement points through manual means. An AI-approach to automate a process is best suited whenever complex and high-volume of nodes (units in a network such as users or devices) and edges (the interaction between these nodes) are involved in a process. Processes where the edges or interactions between the nodes are simple are best served by human-powered option. That's why AI smart services must be created for DDDNs that interact with massive multi-network, user bases. For example, the tedious nature of log files for a server are high volume and perfect for automation.

5. **Complexity.** Tasks that exhibit complexity beyond human comprehension are good candidates for AI. When AI smart services cannot be modeled by math or created by algorithms, DDDNs must engage humans to address this complexity. The DDDNs can study the processes over time to understand when and how to intelligently automate them with the right

AI smart services. For example, an AI service with highly complex computer vision skills still requires human intervention to determine whether a radiology scan is that of a chihuahua or a blueberry muffin.

6. **Creativity.** Today, cognitive processes required for creative tasks such as developing new rules and guidelines, designing new polices, and creating art and music mostly reside with humans and are less likely to be AI-powered. However, with advancements in cognitive learning, the ability of AI to power these creative tasks will improve over the next decade. Humans who create rules are also great at deploying creativity to break them. Cyber security systems are often battle tested by white hats—the good cyber hackers—who use clever, creative ways to beat existing systems. At this point in time, this creativity cannot be replicated by AI smart services—but it will in the future.

7. **Physical presence.** Processes and tasks that require a heavy physical presence to be completed—such as the fine motor skills required when packaging fragile items like glass or even eggs—will most likely require human-powered capabilities. However, processes that put lives in jeopardy—nuclear power plant inspections—serve as great candidates to be automated by AI-powered options. In general, low physical presence requirements play well with AI-powered approaches.

The AI Smart Services Flow Model

We talked about why DDDNs need AI to achieve decision velocity—and when and what processes should be automated with AI. The next step is for DDDNs to actually automate these processes, that is, create these AI smart services. The more decisions

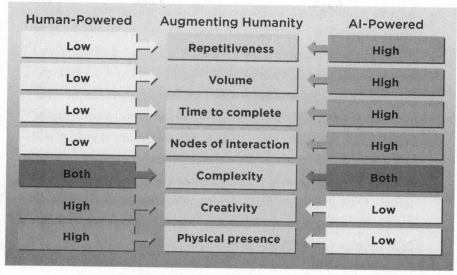

FIGURE 5.2. CANDIDATES FOR AI-DRIVEN AUTOMATION.

that can be intelligently automated via AI smart services, the faster the decision velocity. Every process or journey—from campaign to lead, order to cash, incident to resolution, hire to retire, procure to pay, concept to commercialization, or cash to close—should be intelligently automated to follow the flow illustrated in Figure 5.3.

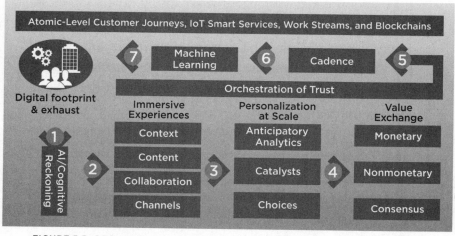

FIGURE 5.3. ORCHESTRATION OF TRUST—INSIDE AI-DRIVEN SMART SERVICES.

- **AI analyzes digital footprints to build anonymous and explicit profiles.** Every individual user or device in the DDDN provides some information. That digital footprint might come from facial analysis, a network IP address, or even one's walking gait. Using AI and cognitive reckoning, systems analyze this data and digital footprint to recognize patterns and create a profile or identity. This means that AI smart services will recognize and know you across different contexts. For example, at 1:50 p.m., I arrive at the lobby of the fifty-story building where I work. Facial analysis and video surveillance (digital footprint) roughly identifies me as "the guy on the tenth floor" (my identity or profile).

- **Immersive experiences enable a natural interaction.** Once the user's identity is established, the AI smart services use contextual information such as geospatial location, time of day, weather, or even heart rate—combined with data about the user's preferences—to deliver immersive and unique experiences. These experiences will include interacting with machines or devices through conversational assistants and text dialogues from the user's mobile phones, via social media, kiosks, and in person. The goal is for the AI smart service to create natural, unique user experiences based on the identity or profile of the user. For example, as I stand in the lobby of the fifty-story building, an AI smart service, having decided I'm the guy on the tenth floor, sends down an elevator to the elevator bank for floors 1 to 20 before I even pressed the elevator button. As I swipe my way in the turnstile to pass security, the DDDN now knows my office is on the tenth floor and a set of immersive experiences are kicked off.

- **Mass personalization at scale delivers digital services.** These unique personalized user experiences delivered at mass scale, will be powered by (1) "anticipatory analytics" or the ability to take a really good guess, which allow users to "skate where the puck will be"; (2) "catalysts"—an offer or trigger for response with the idea of inciting action; and (3) "choices" which allow the user to make their own decisions. Each user will be offered their own experience in contexts depending on their identity or profile, their historical preferences, and their needs at the time.

- **From choose-your-own-adventure** journeys, context-driven offers, and multivariable testing on available choices, the AI smart service will offer statistically driven choices to the user to incite action of some kind. For example, having established my identity and context, the AI smart service anticipates my needs. The system has access to my personal calendar and that of my coworkers. It knows that I've been trying to schedule a meeting with my boss over the past week and that she finally has an opening at 2:00 p.m. She's on the forty-ninth floor. An AI smart service weighs all the probabilities and gives me several choices. The first choice pops up on the elevator console, on my phone, or on my augmented reality glasses: It asks me if I'd like to go to the tenth floor. The AI smart service knows there's a 90 percent chance I'll make that choice. But it also figured out that there's an 83 percent change that I'll want to go to the forty-ninth floor to meet my boss, so it offers that option as well. Having access to my preferences, the AI smart service, knows I like sweets, so decides to test me by offering me a third option: Would I'd like to grab a piece of the leftover dark chocolate birthday cake on floor five? However I answer the A/B test on the birthday cake, it will allow the system to learn more about my behavior and deliver relevant personalized choices in the future.

- **Value exchange completes the orchestration of trust.** Once the user selects a choice and takes action, a "value exchange" cements the transaction. Monetary, nonmonetary, and consensus are three common forms of value exchange. While monetary value exchange might be the most obvious, nonmonetary value exchange (e.g., in exchange for volunteering my data, I receive free access, or I pushed out a *like* in social media and extended that to others in my network) which often provides a compelling form of value. Meanwhile, a simple consensus or agreement between two or multiple parties can also deliver a value exchange. In the elevator example, the consensus would be that in exchange for my data (the information about my behaviors or preferences I shared with the system when I selected one of the three choices it offered), I conveniently got to the right floor without me asking, to a meeting appointment with my boss, or to a free slice of cake. With this step—the value exchange—the AI smart service orchestrates trust among all parties in the network that are interacting with each other.

- **Cadence and feedback continue an AI-powered learning cycle.** Once the AI smart service completes the orchestration of trust—that is, it delivers immersive experiences, personalization at scale, and a value exchange—it moves on to determine its cadence: How often will this AI smart service be deployed? Does the process happen ad hoc and very randomly? Is this a repetitive process? Does the process have a dependency? Once the cadence of the AI smart service is established, the DDDN applies machine learning to discover patterns and teach the AI smart service how to behave in future interactions.

- **Machine learning delivers digital feedback loops and enables the autonomous enterprise.** The AI smart service learns from every transaction to understand how to improve itself. As it does, the precision decisions it produces become more and more autonomous.

Achieving Decision Velocity AI Smart Services

The path to automating processes to achieve decision velocity will follow a maturity model. Decision velocity will be exponentially improved when DDDNs can run fully automated AI smart services. It will take time to build these autonomous AI smart services but their development will rapidly progress throughout the decade. When they are running, DDDNs will deliver signal intelligence services or raw information feeds that are continuous (that is they never stop), auto-compliant (they know how to follow the latest regulations), self-healing (they can repair themselves), self-learning, and self-aware (they sense their surroundings in multiple dimensions). The digital giants who move the fastest along the five levels of autonomous DDDNs have the best chance of emerging as duopolies.

The five levels of autonomous DDDNs are shown in Figure 5.4.

LEVEL 1. BASIC AUTOMATION

The basic automation of AI smart services begins with the automation of tasks, workflows, and remote systems. These capabilities are in place in many enterprises today. DDDNs start with

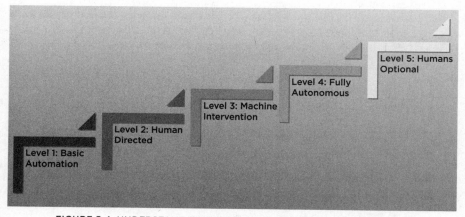

FIGURE 5.4. UNDERSTAND FIVE LEVELS OF AUTONOMOUS NETWORKS.

basic process automation tools such as BPM, manual instrumentation and control, and intelligent workflow automation. Humans still control and guide many manual steps.

LEVEL 2. HUMAN DIRECTED

Human-directed automation of business processes pairs humans with machine. At this level, humans direct the major decisions, while the minor decisions are automated over time as AI smart services are created to learn from human behavior. This represents the current state-of-the-art approach. The tools needed to get to this level of automation include robotic process automation, process mining tools, journey orchestration tools, machine learning algorithms, and natural language processing.

LEVEL 3. MACHINE INTERVENTION

At this level, DDDNs deliver automation with occasional machine intervention, where humans can still override a judgment call by an AI system. The approaches that are used in this level include cognitive applications, neural networks, GANS models, contextual decisions, and next-best-actions. In Level 3, humans are still on standby, but are hands-off for periods of time.

LEVEL 4. FULLY AUTONOMOUS

Level 4 DDDNs have most processes completely automated. The DDDNs presume that the machines can deliver full automation but not sentience through their AI smart services. These capabilities are not available as I write this but will emerge in late 2023. Techniques that are used in this level include full automation of processes, self-learning, self-healing, and self-securing. In level 4, DDDNs are fully automated.

LEVEL 5. HUMANS OPTIONAL

Level 5 DDDNs achieve full sentience and humans may no longer be needed. These DDDNs will emerge in 2030 and deliver full autonomous sentience, empowering precision decisions at scale. In addition to all the Level 4 capabilities, these machines can do everything on their own and have achieved self-awareness. At this level, humans are fully optional.

Focus on Humanizing AI

As you begin deploying AI to create AI smart services and achieve decision velocity, you must keep some ethical considerations in mind. While achieving a uniform set of ethics may seem insurmountable, five principles will help facilitate the humanization of AI smart services and provide appropriate checks and balances (see Figure 5.5). Your AI smart services should be:

1. **Transparent.** Transparency requires that algorithms, attributes, and correlations should be open to inspection by all participants.

2. **Explainable.** Humans should be able to understand how AI systems come to their contextual decisions.

3. **Reversible.** You must be able to reverse what the AI system learns and adjust as needed.

4. **Trainable.** AI systems must have the ability to learn from humans and other systems.

5. **Human-led.** All decisions should begin and end with human decision points.

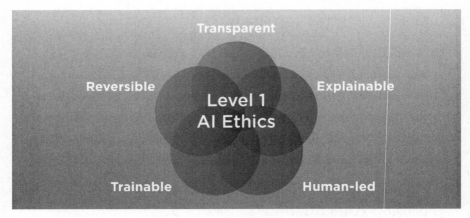

FIGURE 5.5. FIVE PILLARS FOR LEVEL 1 AI ETHICS FOCUS ON HUMANIZING AI.

Honeywell Forge Sets the Stage for Industrial IoT Duopolies

Originally known as Honeywell Connected Enterprise, Honeywell Forge is a multi-sided network platform built for industrial verticals such as buildings, aircraft, plants, cybersecurity, and workforce solutions—and a perfect example of a DDDN that achieved data supremacy and decision velocity. Since 2018, the company has pursued the creation of a comprehensive industrial IoT platform that delivers software and analytics for industrial companies. This open platform facilitates the upstream collection, platform analysis, and downstream delivery of signal intelligence. David Trice, general manager of Honeywell Forge, noted in interviews that the system has to remain open as there are a lot of different analytical models, products, and software inside buildings, industrial plants, and aircrafts. The operational infrastructure used to collect data must support the analytical systems in the back end of the platform.

"Companies tend to spend a lot on analytics, but few get the results they're looking for. Many providers don't have the historical data and insights to apply to their analytics. They don't know the theoretical maximums or how to get there," Darius Adamczyk, CEO of Honeywell Forge explained. "It takes first-hand knowledge in the lab and in real life. For example, if you want to know the shortest distance between two destinations, that's a math formula. The second type of data is empirical—weather, no-go zones and other restraints in getting from A to B. The third type is big data. Factors you get from collected data: how ambient temperatures and other factors affect your model. Not a fundamental yield, but a maximum yield. What happens when deskless workers don't follow maintenance workflows exactly. At Honeywell, we feel it's critical to combine big data with industry knowledge and physical, chemical and empirical knowledge."[5]

As with all good DDDNs, Honeywell Forge has partnered with other companies to deliver solutions on top of their platform. SAP Cloud for Real Estate partnered with Honeywell to deliver a unified dashboard for building sustainability and utilization. The Honeywell Forge Real Estate Operations is an SAP Endorsed Business Application built on the SAP Cloud. The result is a joint go-to-market industry solution bringing together and building operational data from electrical, lighting, security services, and HVAC maintenance with business data on utilization, maintenance, and leasing.

Using this big data together with analytical models, machine intelligence, and artificial intelligence techniques, Honeywell Forge can move customers from planned maintenance cycles to just-in-time maintenance capabilities. Customers can predict when a chiller will die, or an exhaust fan will break, or how often an elevator or escalator will need downtime. Over time this signal intelligence helps customers identify patterns to drive down maintenance costs. Understanding how often a piece of equipment will break and the impact of the downtime on the business helps automate prioritization of incidents. The ability to understand these maintenance costs help companies improve cash deployment, allocate capital for depreciation, staff for common break/fix scenarios, maximize procurement of repair parts and maintenance services, and even renegotiate power purchase agreements.

Honeywell is now set to be in a position to deliver what GE Digital had promised: the ability to build a digital industrial solution to modernize legacy systems. The leadership team's recognition that data supremacy and decision velocity is key to success allows Honeywell to battle Siemens, ABB, GE, and others for duopoly dominance in key industrial verticals.

Conclusion

Digital giants' quest to achieve decision velocity will become more and more competitive. As the rate of decision-making powered by AI increases, the battle for high-quality data will intensify. Digital giants will vie to build the most connected and expansive DDDNs they can. The push to build a more precise DDDN is the heart of every digital giant's business model and what every organization will invest in, optimize, and defend. This insatiable appetite for data and the infinite creation of insights will drive the autonomous era, an era where decision velocity determines the future winners and losers.

6

DESIGN FOR A
LONG-TERM MINDSET

In 1972, Walter Mischel, a Stanford University professor ran an experiment on delayed gratification. The study gave children a simple choice: take one small reward—a marshmallow or pretzel stick—immediately or wait fifteen minutes without eating the first reward to receive a second one. Years later, Mischel and his team went back to study how the children who managed to wait in order to receive a second treat had developed. Mischel discovered that those kids who delayed gratification had better life outcomes based on body mass index (BMI), SAT scores, educational attainment, leadership, and other factors.[1]

Today's CEOs often face a similar dilemma to those kids in the experiment: Do they go for the short-term reward—showing quarter-to-quarter progress and immediately satisfying shareholders—or do they delay gratification by making long-term strategic moves such as investing in research, funding more capital projects, pursuing growth, and initiating management restructuring when competitors are retrenching? A 2019 McKinsey study showed that from 2001 to 2014, companies that "operated for the long term achieved revenues 47 percent higher and earnings 36 percent higher than short-term counterparts did."[2] Leaders of data giants intuitively know that playing the long game pays off. They have a clear understanding of the positive impact of delayed gratification, so they routinely invest for long-term, higher quality revenue streams at the expense of missing short-term quarterly profits.

Unfortunately, few CEOs today have the luxury to shift from a short-term to a long-term mindset. While the average tenure of CEOs among the S&P 500 slightly increased from 7.3 years in 2008 to 10 years in 2018, the tenure of large cap CEOs has decreased.[3] A recent Equilar study showed that the median tenure of a CEO was just five years in 2017.[4] Other recent CEO studies in the past five years also show the median tenure of the CEO to be between four and five years. And Challenger, Gray & Christmas reported a total of 1,160 CEOs in the U.S. had left, resigned, or were fired in the first nine months of 2019. That number was 13 percent higher than all of 2018.[5] In general, the trend of short-tenured CEOs reflects a lack of patience by investors who are looking for short-term performance. If CEOs don't deliver it, they have to move on.

This quest for short-term yield often hinders a company's ability to invest for long-term growth. Over the past decade, leaders have had to deal with a flood of private equity and activist raiders with short-term stock manipulation agendas. Many of these raiders strip the firm of key assets to bolster returns for equity investors while piling on significant amounts of debt. For example, in the 2010s, these raiders encouraged companies to unload their real estate assets and rent back office space in order to pay out dividends to shareholders. Those that followed suit showed short-term growth in quarterly earnings, boosting their stock price and market capitalization—for the time being. However, several quarters later, they were saddled with mountains of debt and new rent obligations, leaving long-term shareholders in the dust. Focused on short-term quarterly performance, they fail to invest in research and development, technology infrastructure, and capital equipment—the kinds of investments that yield long-term growth.

While most organizations must face their boards' and investors' thirst for short-term, quarter-to-quarter margin improvements, leaders of digital giants find ways to focus on the long term. Following the lead of some rapidly growing startups in the technology sector, digital giants focus on performance metrics that allow room for both growth and profitability, and they invest in the future by *over*-investing in technology and R&D. Their leaders also engage in a dynamic kind of leadership and gravitate to governance models that allow them to achieve their long-term visions. If you want to build a DDDN and become a data giant, you will have to as well.

Foster a Growth Mindset with the Rule of 40

Growth is key to building a successful DDDN. But building a massive user base is expensive and takes time. To get it done, you must follow the strategy of well-funded, high growth startups and adopt a winner-takes-all mentality. You must invest in customer acquisition as fast as you can and take as much market share as you can. As Peter Thiel, the legendary co-founder of PayPal, Palantir, and Founders Fund pointed out, competition is for losers.[6] Once you are in the lead, you can set a price that delivers high margins and not have to participate in a competitive market.

Now, this approach is bound to lose money at first, so it takes a long-term vision to execute it. If you are an existing company, how do you pitch it to your board? By advocating that your organization follow the Rule of 40 when measuring performance.

The need to increase investment to drive growth, support rapid expansion, and fuel go-to market strategies are often at odds with profitability. So in a quest to balance rapid growth *and* increased profitability, startups (especially the software-as-a-service or SaaS kind) have adopted the rule that a company's revenue growth rate added to the profitability margin should be equal to or greater than 40 percent. This rule has proven a good metric of performance, showing that growth and profitability can coexist at scale. Our own studies of over a hundred high growth tech startups consistently show a median between 39 to 41 percent achievement over the past 10 years.[7]

How do you work out the rule of 40 in your organization? There are many approaches to measuring the growth rate, but the most common are either annual recurring revenue (ARR)— primarily used by early stage software as a service startups—or year-over-year GAAP revenue growth percentage, typically used by more mature organizations. Measuring profitability margin is a bit trickier as there are multiple ways to do so. The five most common are unlevered free cash flow, EBIDTA, cash from operations, operating income, and net change in cash. EBIDTA seems to be the easiest to use when comparing public companies.

However you measure growth and profit margin, their percentages added should exceed 40 percent to make sure you are properly investing in growing your DDDN at the rate it needs to become a digital giant. For most high-growth startups, the first few years can be in the triple digits. Historical averages show that high-growth companies with over $50 million in revenue at year five or six of operation will tend to operate at 40 percent or greater growth rate. Some of the well-known startups to achieve the Rule of 40 include Livongo Health, Salesforce, Shopify, Splunk, and Workday.

Over-invest in R&D and Technology

One of the hallmarks of digital giants is that they invest heavily on innovation and technology. In many cases, they fund research that may never result in a breakthrough or a new product.

However, they apply whatever they learn from their R&D efforts to improve processes or create tangential offerings that sometimes lead to a blockbuster. Organizations with a long-term mindset always invest for the future.

That's why a good indicator of a long-term mindset is both the amount of research and development an organization invests in and the percentage of revenue earmarked in its budget for that purpose. Recent studies show that the top twenty-five R&D spenders (see Figure 6.1) mostly concentrate in three industries— auto, pharma, and high technology. These industries have traditionally competed on innovation so they have made the most significant investments in the world's total innovation budget. Companies such as Intel and Facebook spend up to 20 percent of their revenues on R&D. The parent company of Google, Alphabet, spends up to 15 percent of its revenues on R&D.

Amazon.com: US$22.62bn	**Apple:** US$11.581bn	**Novartis:** US$8.51bn	**Robert Bosch:** US$7.121bn
Alphabet: US$16.225bn	**Roche:** US$10.804bn	**Ford Motor:** US$8bn	**Honda Motor:** US$7.079bn
Volkswagen: US$15.772bn	**Johnson & Johnson:** US$10.554bn	**Facebook:** US$7.754bn	**Sanofi:** US$6.571bn
Samsung: US$15.311bn	**Daimler:** US$10.396bn	**Pfizer:** US$7.657bn	**Bayer:** US$6.194bn
Microsoft: US$14.735bn	**Merck US:** US$10.208bn	**BMW:** US$7.33bn	**Siemens:** US$6.103bn
Huawei: US$13.601bn	**Toyota Motor:** US$10.02bn	**General Motors:** US$7.3bn	**Oracle:** US$6.091bn
Intel: US$13.098bn			

FIGURE 6.1. TOP 25 R&D SPENDERS IN 2018.

While shareholders and investors often scrutinize a company's percentage of spending on R&D and try to hold companies to "established" benchmarks (such as no more than 2 percent of revenue on technology and innovation for low-margin industries), the companies that spend more on R&D and innovation often lead their industries. Case in point, the digital giants in the "four comma" club—Amazon, Apple, Microsoft, and Google—make up the top ten in R&D spend. It's no wonder these digital giants are duopolies in their own right. Apple has a duopoly position on smartphones against Samsung. Microsoft is battling Amazon for cloud computing and is a dominant player in the operating systems wars. Google's dominance in search has it pitted against Facebook for digital advertising. These digital giants are investing in adjacent areas of innovation in order to break their dominant business models and optimize for monetization.

A closer look at companies that spend specifically on technology and information technology (IT) shows that the retail, financial services, and tech industries are leading in this regard. While there isn't always a direct correlation between spending on IT and long-term success, there is evidence that spending disproportionately more on IT can take out the competition. Amazon's dominance in the retail and e-commerce industry is one data point. The digital giant has spent $35.9 billion on IT and R&D—a bit over 40 percent of its revenues on long-term investment. The average retailer, on the other hand, spends just 1 percent of its revenues on IT and maybe 3 percent on innovation. Digital giants over-invest. So should you if you want to dance with them.[8]

Funding Your DDDN: All Money Is Not Created Equal

Existing companies building a DDDN often consider whether they should take funding from private equity and buyout firms. Not short on cash, the buyout industry has spent years building up its dry powder—money that investors have committed to private equity funds that hasn't yet been spent. According to data provider Preqin Ltd., as of June 2020 that pile was at a record $1.45 trillion globally, excluding venture-capital funds.[9] As a result, the players in the buyout industry are eager to deploy this cash in as many new investments as possible, but lack significant interest in pouring new money into existing investments.

Without doubt, private equity firms have a place in turn-arounds and the creation of future digital giants. But you must be careful to engage with the right PE firm. To take or not take private equity comes down to the business model of the particular PE firm you are courting. Some PE firms have the appetite for long-term approaches, but most lack the gene for long-term thinking. They often give companies they buy out three to four years to initiate a turnaround before they repackage them for sale or for a shot back at the public market for funding.

Often PE firms raid and asset-strip the value of a company by having their assets and real estate pared off as special dividends funded by a mysterious category known as "leveraged loans," basically a form of recapitalization through borrowing. Asset stripping is no laughing matter. Since 2016, $15.7 billion has been asset-stripped out of companies, loading companies up with risky debts, which banks facilitate and then unload on mutual funds, pension funds, and other institutional investors in the quest for yield. In 2019, the total outstanding amount of leveraged loans was just under $2 trillion dollars, with $1.3 trillion held by institutional investors.[10] These leveraged loans are often made to companies in the junk-rated status. When the economy is great, these tactics can work out. However, in the post-pandemic market, many companies could not recover.

During the pandemic, we saw several high-profile examples of this, including J. Crew, Neiman Marcus, and Toys "R" Us. In each of these cases, PE firms saddled the companies with debt while stripping them of their assets. During good economic times, many sounded the alarm but were massively ignored. There wasn't much appetite to regulate the process or go after the fund owners that abused this practice. With great cash flow, continued payments on debt, and demonstrable growth, these companies could do no wrong. But in the downturn, investors realized that growing the stock value in the short run at the expense of the company's long-term financial health was detrimental. These moves left these companies too extended, too vulnerable, and too rigid to survive a major crisis, like the economic shutdown forced by the pandemic.

Should you take PE firms' money to fund your DDDN, you must be very explicit and careful when working with them. While maintaining financial discipline on costs may be helpful, you must also limit the amount of debt and leveraged loans you incur. In addition, you must protect your largest assets and cash so you can retake markets and be prepared for the long term. Do not let PE firms bleed you dry. Especially when creating a joint venture startup, you must be watchful—venture capital firms, institutional investors, and family offices (private wealth-management advisories that cater to ultra-rich families) may prove to have more of a long-term mindset than PE firms.

Embrace a Dynamic Leadership Style

Making the decision to invest in long-term growth and innovation—or to forgo funding from PE—in a business landscape obsessed with short-term results requires more than a strong leader. It requires a different approach to leading altogether.

Today's leadership models center on either responsive or responsible styles of leading. Responsive leadership is characterized by agility and flexibility in decision making, while responsible leadership is characterized by structured and rule-abiding approaches. But the continual over-emphasis and under-emphasis on one type of leadership style over the other is no longer relevant for the challenges that most leaders will have to deal with in the age of duopolies.

Organizations are facing digital disruption from non-traditional competitors, emerging technologies, and new business models like they've never seen before. Technologies such as AI and robotics are having a major impact on the future of work and will play a key role in the development of policies that address humanity in a digital age. As the global system is challenged by a confluence of political, economic, societal, technological, environmental, and legislative forces, it will demand leaders who can bring generations together, create inclusiveness in growth opportunities, and bridge cultural and economic divides. In the age of duopolies, the leaders who will drive their organizations to success are those who can manage the pace of change required not only for survival, but also for cultural agility—leaders who are both responsive and responsible and who take a dynamic approach to leading.

These dynamic leaders exhibit five core traits that have always been essential for leadership. These traits do not change with time or business trends. If you want to lead a digital giant onto a duopoly stage, you must hone these traits and make them a part of your DNA (see Figure 6.2):

1. **Integrity.** Great leaders have strong moral principles, demonstrate honesty, and uphold honor.

2. **Inspiration.** Great leaders stimulate and draw people toward ideas, concepts, and actions.

3. **Inclusiveness.** Great leaders bring people together from different backgrounds and points of view to create equal opportunities.

4. **Authenticity.** Great leaders are genuine about who they are and what they stand for.

5. **Transparency.** Great leaders hold themselves accountable and provide clarity on their decisions and actions.

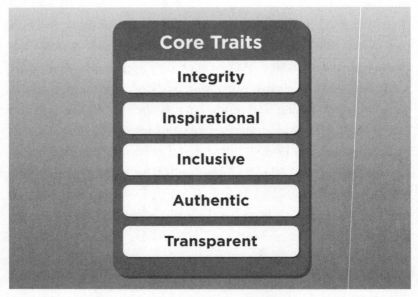

FIGURE 6.2. FIVE IMMUTABLE CORE TRAITS NEVER CHANGE FOR GREAT LEADERS.

But dynamic leaders don't stop there. They also master and modulate between responsive and responsible approaches to seven key areas of leadership in order to achieve an effective, contextually appropriate, right-for-the-moment leadership style. They balance their approach to carry out their organizations' missions, long-term goals, and objectives.

Once you've honed the five core traits, it's time to finesse these responsive and responsible approaches to leading. There are seven key areas in leadership (see Figure 6.3) and for each of them leaders can take either a responsive or a responsible approach:

1. **Decision making.** Decision making is about assimilating the key information to make a choice or a set of choices. When

leaders approach decision making in a responsible way, they tend to be "decisive." Decisive leaders make bold moves, come to quick conclusions, and rapidly communicate their course of action. But when leaders approach decision-making from a responsive way they tend to be "pensive," that is they actively seek input, showcase the questions being asked, and consider all points of view as they deliberate to a decision. When deciding to pursue a decision-making process in a decisive versus a pensive way, consider the following question: Is arriving at a rapid and clear decision more important in this instance than following a thoughtful methodology to making the decision?

2. **Demeanor.** Demeanor is the way leaders presents themselves. When leaders approach their demeanor in a responsible way, they tend to be composed. They appear to be logical and they refrain from showing their emotions. However, leaders taking a responsive approach exhibit a passionate demeanor and transparently show their emotions, rally the troops based on their mood, and respond to other people's feelings. When deciding whether to present your demeanor in a responsible or responsive manner, consider the following question: Would a composed presence outweigh a passionate emotional manner?

3. **Goals and objectives.** Goals refer to general guidelines and aspirations while objectives describe specific approaches and implementing steps to achieve those goals. Objectives can be measured, are well-defined, and must be met by a specific date. When leaders take a responsible approach, they value collective goals and objectives by prioritizing the community and its broader interests over that of a single individual.

Leaders who take a responsive approach focus on personalizing the goals and objectives around an individual and ensuring that individual has the freedom to determine his or her destiny. When thinking about collective versus individual goals and objectives, contemplate whether or not you should think about the larger group instead of the individual's self-interest.

4. **Policy and actions.** Policy and actions are the tools used to guide work. When leaders take a responsible approach to policy and actions, they value principled rules. Policies and rules are taken seriously and those who fail to follow them face scorn, punishment, and negative engagement. Leaders who take a responsive approach to policy and actions focus on adaptive approaches around the individual and ensuring the individual has the freedom to determine their destiny. When thinking about your approach to policy and action—principled versus adaptive—you must ask whether or not you should enforce strict rules, or take an adaptive approach to the rules enforcement.

5. **Motivational approach.** Motivational approach describes how leaders inspire others to get work done. When leaders take a responsible approach they are often demanding. Followers can expect the company to meet and beat standards with a high degree of rigor and discipline. Responsible leaders make clear hard targets and rewards and push teams to beat benchmarks. Leaders who choose a responsive approach, on the other hand, apply compassion and leverage their trust in their team to engender good performance, empower self-directing teams, and appeal to individuals at a personal level. You must determine when a demanding

versus a compassionate motivational approach will work. Should you push hard for more or will reaching out with more compassion result in better esprit de corps?

6. **Performance expectations.** Performance expectations clarify the requirements an employee ought to meet, including work results, behaviors, and actions. Leaders who take a responsible approach to performance expectations seek accountability. Expectations are explicit and applied equally to all employees. Rewards and punishments are also explicit. Responsive leaders, on the other hand, take an empathetic approach and try to match expectations to an individual's ability, taking into account their strengths and weaknesses. When deciding to set performance expectations, you must ask: Is a broad policy-driven and results-driven style more important than a personalized approach to achievement?

7. **Execution style.** Execution style refers to how leaders prioritize what work gets done. Responsible leadership emphasizes a focused approach, proactively identifying market opportunities, prioritizing strategies to achieve goals, and identifying a fixed investment timeline. Responsive leaders take a more opportunistic approach; they decide what work gets done based on the current environment and they prioritize based on what's the best option at that particular point in time. Leaders making a decision on which execution style to take must ask: Should you emphasize a laser focus on a task or prepare for situational awareness?

In the past, each of the individual approaches to these key areas, like taking a "decisive" or "pensive" approach have often been used to simplify leadership qualities and to describe traits of

Leaders must find harmony and master balance among 14 foundational attributes

Responsible	Master balance among 14 foundational attributes	Responsive
Decisive	Decision making	Pensive
Composed	Demeanor	Passionate
Collective	Goals and objectives	Individual
Principled	Policy and actions	Adaptive
Demanding	Motivational approach	Compassionate
Accountable	Performance expectations	Empathetic
Focused	Execution style	Opportunistic

FIGURE 6.3. RESPONSIBLE AND RESPONSIVE APPROACHES TO THE SEVEN KEY LEADERSHIP AREAS.

a great leader. For example, great generals have been known to be demanding. Leaders of freedom movements have been shown to be principled. But other great leaders have also won over people not by being demanding but with compassion or by being adaptive. This one-dimensional approach to describing leadership leads to an imbalanced understanding of what it takes to succeed as a leader in the coming age of duopolies.

By adopting this yin-yang style of leadership, leaders can account for a more complex reality, attenuate a leadership approach as needed, and foster their long-term mindset by adapting to changing conditions (see Figure 6.4). Many leaders have invested time and effort perfecting an extreme on any one of the seven dimensions. By understanding when and how to modulate between the two, leaders gain new techniques that give them the confidence to address an increasingly complex reality.

Success at the leadership level will translate into much broader organizational values and capabilities and enable leaders to master a long-term mindset. For example, if a CEO knows that they will be able to renew or extend their three-year contract to five or seven years, they will double down on infrastructure and innovation investments. Hiring and recruiting will focus on more expensive, higher-quality hires. Customers and prospects will gain a sense of stability and longevity in the sales posture and choose to become strategic partners. However, if a leader is playing a short-term game of twenty-four to thirty-six months, his or her goal will be reflected in short-term gains at long-term cost. That leader will make minimal investments in infrastructure and innovation. Hiring will be sporadic and not strategic. Customers will feel that the relationship with the company is transactional and not strategic.

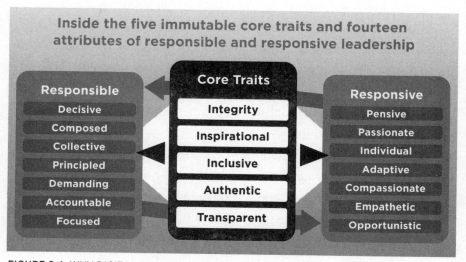

FIGURE 6.4. WHY DIGITAL TRANSFORMATION REQUIRES A DYNAMIC LEADERSHIP MODEL.

Install Benevolent Governance or Dominant Ownership

Of course, you might embrace a dynamic leadership style to lead your organization with the kind of long-term mindset required to build a DDDN and still be derailed by activist shareholders and investors who are more interested in short-term profits. To avoid this fate, you might want to look to founder-led organizations such as Airbnb, Atlassian, Crowdstrike, Facebook, Google, Lyft, Pinterest, Shopify, Snap, Tesla, The Trade Desk, and Zoom. These companies have "super voting" governance structures that allow their founders or CEOs to build data giants focused on both growth *and* innovation and that encourage a long-term mindset.

Often known as dual-class share structures, they assign one group of shareholders, let's call it Class A, more votes a share. For example, Class A members get ten votes per share while another group, Class B, may get one vote per share. At a company with 100,000 shares where 10 percent of them are Class A, this class of shareholders would have 10,000 shares but 100,000 votes. Class B holders with 100,000 shares would have 100,000 votes. Thus, Class A members would only need 10,001 shares to secure a majority. That's how this model enables one class—usually company founders and their close networks, such as the founding CEO—to exert tremendous voting control, even if they give up more ownership in shares.

Companies that set up a dual class structure get the best of both worlds: They have access to the public equity markets for financing but maintain control of their companies. They have the luxury to make long-term decisions and take strategic positions when compared to rivals who operate with a standard governance model. A dual class structure protects an entrepreneurial management team from the whims of ordinary shareholders, activist groups, and social shaming organizations with a political agenda. For example, Mark Zuckerberg has been able to hold his ground on certain free speech policies— particularly the extent to which Facebook is willing to fact check politicians' posts and political ads—despite activist groups demanding Facebook do so. Supervoting majorities also protect against hostile takeovers by private equity firms or competitors when stock prices are low amidst a quarterly setback, market downturn, or bad product cycle. Startups such as Lyft, where founders kept a supervoting majority, were able to survive dips in their IPOs and continue to invest in the long-term without having to worry about being sold off below their initial market valuation.

While this governance approach is quite popular with tech startups and digital giants, other traditional companies have set up this arrangement for years. For example, Warren Buffett's company offers a Class B share for Berkshire Hathaway that has 1/30th the value of the Class A shares and only 1/200th of the voting rights. The Ford family has a dual-class super voting stock structure that enables a 4 percent stake in the company to control 40 percent of the shareholder voting power.

To be fair, there are downsides to benevolent dictatorship governance structures just as there are with benevolent dictatorships. Some leaders end up engaging in nepotism. For instance, WeWork CEO Adam Neumann purportedly convinced the board to buy a matching private jet for his wife Rebekah as a gesture of "fairness" pre-IPO. Other leaders lose touch with their employees and key shareholders, A few companies have had to deal with crazy leaders. In some cases, a benevolent dictator leader overstays his or her tenure past the point where he or she has the brilliance and tenacity to lead. Yahoo's legendary founders Jerry Yang and David Filo over-extended their stay as the market shifted from ad networks to media properties. Because Yahoo was not structured as a dual class company, its board was able to bring in new leadership. In those cases where the leader can no longer take the company to the next level, swift decision making on a sale of the company, replacement of key leaders, or establishing critical partnerships can be made, should that leader come to the same conclusions.

For the most part, however, digital giants leverage these super voting, benevolent governance structures to realize their vision and scale investment in their DDDN. Unfettered long-term investment strategies allow leadership teams to design for exponential growth, build the right infrastructure to scale regardless of market conditions, and deliver on decision velocity. They know they have the stability to execute these long-term strategies required to win in the age of duopolies.

Creating a DDDN takes time and requires investment not just for growing the network but in costly AI technology that enables decision velocity. For the build-from-the-ground-up digital giants, this corporate governance approach will support a long-term mindset. But for established companies trying to transform into digital giants, the best approach may be to establish a separate independent business unit that has the freedom to act like a built-from-the-ground-up digital giant. Should that option not be available, the chances of success quickly diminish—unless the board and its shareholders are replaced with forward-looking members who understand the charter required to succeed as a digital giant.

Long-Term Mindset Spawns a Digital Giant in India

The importance of having a long-term vision and mindset to elevate your DDDN into a digital giant is well evidenced in the story of Reliance Jio and its founding CEO, Mukesh Ambani. Launched in September of 2016, Jio has emerged as the number one telecom operator in terms of revenue and market share.[11] The competition for the 1.15 billion mobile user market in India is now down to Bharti Airtel Ltd, Vodafone, and Jio. From developing innovative low-cost handsets to affordable data plans, Ambani has guided the company to make the long-term investments necessary to take the once stodgy multinational conglomerate out of the industrial age.

At the heart of this emerging digital giant is Jio's DDDN with a massive 400 million users on its telecom network.[12] The multi-sided network brings social networks and commerce together through tech partnerships with social media companies such as Facebook's WhatsApp unit. These digital services and goods monetization models work in concert with Jio's subscription models. In time, Jio will likely build an ad network as well. Ambani's vision is to stitch his digital empire of 400 million users from his telecom network to Jio Studios—its in-house marketing and content agency—for content, to Network 18—its in-house media and communications studio—for media, to Reliance Retail for commerce, to Reliance Global Logistics for last mile-delivery, and to set-top boxes and voice assistants that allow home automation. Essentially, Ambani wants to forever change how you buy food, watch content, connect with family and friends, read the news, and are targeted for promotions in India.

Ambani is in a good position to drive his vision. Jio's parent company, Reliance Industries, was started in 1973 by his father, Dhirajlal Hirachand Ambani and his second cousin Chambaklai Dmarni. They began exporting spices to Yemen and importing polyester yarn to India. Emerging as the "polyester king," over the next four decades the company expanded its reach into many industries, including energy, petrochemical, natural resources, life sciences, and telecommunications. The Ambani family has held on to a little more than 46.3 percent of the stock, with the remainder held by public shareholders.

As founding CEO of Jio, Ambani has exerted an owner's mentality to the business, fine-tuning costs while making big bets into new, exponential technologies such as the early adoption of voice over LTE which will give him an advantage when 5G networks come into play. Having dominant ownership position allows him to raise foreign capital from outside investors and to weather the toughest criticisms of his choice to over-invest in technology and R&D. The success of Jio since 2016 shows the growth mindset that only owner operators can deliver for the long-term success of the company.

7

PARTNER OR BE PUNISHED

Part one of this book outlined how an organization can become a digital giant by building its own data-driven digital network. But as we've seen, building a DDDN is neither easy nor cheap. So I'll explain how organizations can choose a different path to becoming a digital giant: by partnering with others and forming joint venture startups that craft and orchestrate their own DDDN.

What happens to those organizations who ignore the threat of digital giants, chose to neither build their own DDDN or partner with others to build one, and continue to focus on short-term, quarter-to-quarter survival? They will steadily face declines in market positions and erosion of margins from both traditional competitors and those out of left field. With 63 percent of the Fortune 500 merged, acquired, or gone bankrupt since 2000, the age of duopolies will hasten their demise.

Organizations will have to make a crucial decision: should I build, partner, or be punished?

Those who choose to form joint ventures will have to pick the right business model and partners and will need to avoid the typical pitfalls that derail partnerships and consortiums.

How to Craft a Joint Venture Partnership (the Right Way)

Over the years, I've encountered countless organizations that decided to join others to form a joint DDDN only after their attempts to go at it on their own failed miserably. This happens more frequently than you think: A company pays lip service to building a costly DDDN, grossly underfunds it, then when the initiative fails to get any traction, it scraps it for good. A breathtaking amount of money is wasted in the process and nothing is left to show for it.

Take the hypothetical example of a commercial real estate firm that wants to invest in a smart-building data-driven digital network (DDDN). A forward-looking chief experience officer has been advocating for years for the need to make this long-term investment. He finally receives approval for $150 million over three years to fund a demo project. Although the real capital investment cost of building a DDDN is actually in the range of $1.5 billion to $2 billion, the company is proud to announce the $150 million initiative. The CEO is lauded for his innovative and bold stance, and the organization sees an increase in stock price for its defining digital vision. Three years later, the CEO makes his stock-price goals and leaves to collect a bonus. In short, the executive team pumped the stock for success and then cashed out. They faked a digital giant!

Yet sadly, at the end of the three years, the project is nowhere near completion, a lot of money has been wasted, and investment has drained away. The team that was building the DDDN is disbanded and spread out into the organization. The incoming CEO, saddled with even more extreme EBIDTA targets for earnings per share (EPS), has moved on to the next management consulting trend she hopes will give her the next boost in stock price.

Instead of making a steady series of long-term investments in their company, the commercial real estate organization will have completed hundreds of million dollars' worth of stock buybacks and dividend payouts and have conducted mergers to get to its new and even higher EPS target instead. Even worse, investors take the money they stripped away from these cash-cow companies to fund billions for startups in the smart-buildings space that compete with *their* cash cows.

This is the fate that befalls most companies that have tried to build a DDDN on their own. But it doesn't have to be.

Building DDDN with others allows an organization to create a DDDN with less investment than if they had each tried to build a DDDN on their own—but with a force multiplier in terms of the impact on the market. To successfully form a joint venture, they must be clear about why they want to partner and what each partner brings to the table.

IDENTIFY KEY BUSINESS MODELS

The first step is for those seeking to craft partnerships for building a DDDN to identify the key business and monetization models behind their venture. Similar to building a DDDN on one's own, partners must articulate the underlying rationale for their DDDN: How is it going to generate value? Let's take the example of how a joint venture goes about creating a commercial smart-building DDDN. As they consider business models to pursue, members of this venture would have several options.

In the first model, the DDDN's ability to match available inventory of commercial real estate (supply) with the demand for corporate real estate and facility needs would allow commercial real estate operators to provide dynamic pricing. For example, mall facilities could create pop-up experiences in slow summer months, while charging kiosks 200 to 300 percent more per square feet during peak holiday season.

In another model, the network effect of managing commercial real estate for thousands of clients in similar utility districts would create opportunities to pre-purchase and renegotiate bulk power contracts based on volume, time of use, and energy efficient investment measures. Alternatively, the joint venture could create a DDDN that allows commercial real estate operators to create opt-in networks among building residents and local store owners to streamline payments, promotional offers, and commerce opportunities. This network could be tied to building security systems and the value-added services would enable local florists, restaurants, and business services establishments to target building occupants based on their needs and past purchase behaviors.

The DDDN could also create a digital ad network. Aided by computer vision surveillance that identifies a building's high traffic areas at peak times, these systems could enable digital smart signage in lobbies, retail establishments, and elevators to match advertising and paid content with the building occupants' demographics. Or the DDDN might monitor energy consumption, water usage, greenhouse gas emissions, waste water effluent, and solar energy generation to help clients achieve, maintain, and exceed green certification. Building monitoring systems would help detect any anomalies such as excess energy consumption or water leaks.

ATTRACT JOINT VENTURE PARTNERS

Once the business and monetization models have been identified, organizations need to evaluate potential partners and consider what skills they bring to the table and where they fit in the value chain. Potential partners can bring intellectual property, membership networks, capital, connections, and talent.

In the case of the real estate organization that wants to build a commercial smart-building DDDN, the real estate organization does not have the technical infrastructure and the technical talent to succeed in delivering a project built around IoT technologies. So, a natural approach would be to attract other partners that bring tech infrastructure and tech talent partners.

The commercial real estate organization may, for example, invite a cloud company such as Alibaba, Amazon, Google, IBM, Microsoft or Oracle to invest $100 million of capital expenditures and handle the technology infrastructure requirements of the joint venture. This would match the organization's initial commitment of $100 million, bringing the total amount of raised funds to $200 million. In parallel, the commercial real estate organization might also court a system integrator such as Accenture, or Deloitte, or IBM Global that can bring the right talent to the mix, and ask them for $50 million investment to design, build, and operate the new venture. While this may seem crazy at first, the vision of building the next digital giant in the commercial real estate market might easily bring cash-rich tech companies and growth-oriented tech talent partners together to invest in the joint venture.

With $250 million in investment to build a smart-building DDDN, the joint venture could go to market on day one with great fanfare. However, at this point, the venture would not be able to defend its market without a wider net of partners. It would need to do one more thing to succeed: With momentum on its side, it would need to tap the main players in the value chain for a $5 million to $10 million innovation investment in exchange for 1 percent of the new venture. So, value chain players such as elevators, building controls, HVAC and air handling, and sensors companies (e.g., ABB, Hitachi, Honeywell, Johnson Controls,

Schneider Electric, Siemens, Thyssenkrupp, United Technologies [Otis], and others) would become investors as well. These companies would be part of the joint venture startup not only as partners, but also as customers. With about $400 million now raised, the DDDN would be truly ready to go to market.

ACHIEVE FIRST-MOVER ESCAPE VELOCITY

Once a business model and the partners are chosen, a new entity emerges. The key is to achieve first-mover advantage, which would place the competitors at a disadvantage from the moment it launches. The genesis of a digital giant via a partnership and a rapid market consolidation can lead to duopolies on day one. Other players might emerge, but they would have a hard time achieving market scale or finding investors willing to battle against the digital giants. Future competition will most likely come from a digital giant from an adjacent industry looking to invade the value chain.

This is how it would play out in the case of the hypothetical commercial smart-building partnership. This joint venture would be one of the biggest announcements in the industry and the new entity would emerge as a first mover on day one. The joint venture's valuation would most likely hover between $2 billion and $3 billion based on the $400 million raised. Institutional investors and shareholders would rush to invest in it. As a result, their capital outflows from competitors would devalue competitor stocks. Competitors would lose massive market capitalization and value. Those organizations who did not partner with the joint venture startup would be punished with lower stock prices by the market.

The new joint venture would be able to attract top talent from its competitors by dangling their richer stock options and the prospect of shaping a new, disruptive entity. This surgical recruiting of top talent in product design, sales, and partnerships would create an immediate brain drain on unprepared competitors. Key customers, indirect transfer of IP, and market momentum would shift to the joint venture startup.

Meanwhile, competitors would respond six months to a year later by announcing their own joint venture startup. They would partner for their cloud infrastructure and tech talent with different partners. Competitors could potentially raise more money for their own partnership. However, the first-mover, new entity would have a 40 to 50 percent plus market share, and, more importantly, it would have most of the innovation dollars in the value chain as investors. Competitors might get 20 to 30 percent of the market and whatever scraps of innovation dollars are left. There would still be likely the No. 2 player, but they'd be unlikely to receive much investment from the value chain.

Between the two players, the market would be most likely over-capitalized and saturated. A third player would have a hard time entering the smart-building market as they would not be able to achieve market scale or find investors willing to battle against the digital giants. For a third competitor to succeed, patient capital and a long view would be required, perhaps only possible if it's backed by a sovereign wealth fund, a family office, or a nontypical investor like Masayoshi "Masa" Son, the CEO of Softbank or Hiroshi "Miki" Mikitani, the CEO of Rakuten, or the Mukesh Ambanis of the World, CEO of Reliance Industries.

11 Best Practices for Successful Joint Venture Startups

While partnerships are a logical approach to orchestrating several parties to pursue a common interest, before you go down the path of creating one to build a DDDN, it's important to know these are notoriously complex to convene, let alone execute. The market is littered with failed consortiums. When addressing complex challenges, partner organizations often fail to make the most rational decisions with the best interests of their organizations. These partnerships typically don't flounder because of a lack of good intent among their participants, but more often due to a misalignment of goals and understanding. The priorities and objectives of each partner shift, increasing the difficulty and lowering the likelihood of success.

In a study of over a hundred partnerships and consortiums, my firm learned a great deal about what makes them work and what doesn't. When we apply these lessons to new joint venture partnerships to build DDDNs, we arrive at eleven best practices for how to avoid failure and how to create a successful joint venture startup (see Figure 7.1):

Factors	Failed Consortiums	New Joint Ventures
Motivation	Assumption of shared interest	Design for self-interest
Focus	Cost savings	Growth and innovation
Design point	Support complete requirements	Minimum viable offering
Market goal	Gain market share	Winner takes all
Monetization model	Transactions	Insight
IP rights	None	Consortium-owned
Investment	Operating funds from P&L	Capital funds
Governance	Federation of consensus	Benevolent dictatorship
Org structure	Rules-based, policy-driven	Agile, fast-moving
P&L	Cost center	Profit center
Exit strategy	Profitable shared service	IPO

FIGURE 7.1. ELEMENTS OF NEW JOINT VENTURE MODELS
BUILDS ON LESSONS LEARNED.

SHIFT FROM SHARED INTERESTS TO SELF-INTEREST

When a consortium lacks a shared purpose among its members, it is at risk of falling apart. The glow of the new partnership fades fast as the priorities of the members change, especially in turbulent times. Organizational objectives change. Leadership changes. The result: As priorities shift for the partners, a lack of motivation or will follows, and with it, the inability for the consortium to make decisions.

In the joint venture model, the motivation of the group should come from a commonwealth of self-interest, where explicit objectives drive the mission of the venture. Every partner must answer the old adage "What's in it for me?" Once those priorities, expectations, and aspirations have been articulated, the joint venture startup is poised to succeed.

SHIFT FROM COST SAVINGS TO GROWTH AND INNOVATION

Most consortia are created to improve operational efficiencies. They prioritize cost-cutting, process optimization, and automating regulatory compliance. But focusing on cost saving and on achieving profitability at scale leads to short-term gain at the expense of long-term pain. As the consortium ages, members often fail to agree on how to invest for the future.

In the joint venture model, growth and innovation should be the focus from the beginning. A growth mindset is essential. With so much investment aggregated into the new entity, members will have the economies of scale to fund whatever innovation is necessary. For example, say the entity needs to acquire a new technology capability that calls for a $1 billion investment. If a hundred members of the joint venture each contribute $10 million, they can fund growth and innovation while keeping the existing business running.

SHIFT FROM FULLY FLEDGED, FULLY FUNCTIONAL TO MINIMUM VIABLE OFFERINGS

Creating a perfected offering with all features and bells and whistles in place takes far too long. And yet, that's what partnerships often end up aiming for. Every member has an exhaustive list of features and requirements they want to see in their offering before it's launched, bogging down the delivery of its first iteration, even in the presence of strong project management.

In the joint venture model, the new entity should apply agile methodologies to deliver a minimum viable offering and then rapidly iterate as market conditions evolve. Get features out as fast as possible while maintaining high quality. The members of the joint venture startup will benefit from faster cycles, more responsive design, and the ability to quickly course correct.

SHIFT FROM GROWING MARKET SHARE TO WINNER-TAKES-ALL MARKET

Once up and running, consortia tend to focus on the slow process of adding members and growing market share while cutting costs. But they miss the larger picture. Growing market share is less important than capturing key anchor partners that capture the rest of the supply chain. That's where they go wrong.

In a joint venture model, the new entity should proactively secure key partners and suppliers across the value chain to lock up strategic networks. The venture partners should strategically invite participants with dominant market share, significant patent portfolios, and top talent. To be successful, their goal should be to dominate the market on day one.

SHIFT FROM TRANSACTIONS TO INSIGHT

Most consortium models focus on increasing profitable transaction volume. But they completely ignore the value of the insight hidden right there in the treasure trove of data they've collected.

In joint venture models, leaders should design the DDDN to automate data collection and analysis, uncover signal intelligence, and deliver timely precision decisions. Their goal should be to move from data to information flows, from information flows to insights, from insights to actions, and from actions to decisions. This data-to-decision flow powers the digital giant.

SHIFT FROM A LACK OF INTELLECTUAL PROPERTY (IP) RIGHTS TO VENTURE-OWNED IP

Joint venture partnerships should have incentives to create new IP. Consortia often do not grant explicit IP rights to their members. When they do, members often find consortium-owned IP restrictions to be onerous. In other cases, consortia intentionally chose an open source model, but it makes monetization of the core IP hard to control.

In a joint venture model, IP rights should be consortium-owned and shared by members who create new IP in order to accelerate the pace of innovation. Partners should be encouraged to build on top of platform IP without fearing patent theft or breach of IP laws. And access to IP should controlled by the venture members and available only to other members.

SHIFT FROM FUNDING VENTURE FROM OPERATING BUDGETS TO CAPITAL BUDGETS

Often consortium members fund their share of their investment in the consortium from operating capital budgets. When they do, they put the consortium at the mercy of the fickle market. CFOs looking to shore up their organization's bottom line often start by cutting funding for consortium-led innovation budgets. Even when legal agreements are in place, inconsistent funding from individual members wreaks havoc on the consortium.

In the joint venture model, members should fund their investment share from capital budgets, freeing up pressure on their

P&L and providing a two- to three-year time frame for success. Capital expenditures are normally better protected by boards and CFOs than operating budgets and are seen through the lens of a long-term mindset. Making these investments over a consistent period of time ensures that long-term venture strategies are adequately funded and supported.

SHIFT FROM CONSENSUS TO BENEVOLENT DICTATOR GOVERNANCE

A lack of strong leadership torpedoes consortiums. They often adopt a consensus governance model, which makes it difficult to make swift and decisive decisions and which hampers progress and decision velocity. Endless policy debates often plague older consortia, especially when their shared mission has evolved over time. The idea that every member has an equal vote may seem egalitarian and a recipe for everyone's interests to be met. But the chances that this governance model leads to failure often outweigh its benefits.

In a joint venture model, strong leadership will ensure the venture can compete with founder-owners or owner-operator competitors. Giving some members super-voting capabilities enables the venture to make swifter decisions, withstand short-term criticism, and make long-term bets. This benevolent dictator governance model requires a dynamic leader who can steer the venture in the right direction.

SHIFT FROM RIGID TO AGILE ORGANIZATIONAL STRUCTURES

While well-intentioned, consortia that are run under strict rule-based policies often fail to respond to market conditions or to foster innovation. One example might be a rule that does not allow the consortium to reinvest profits into a new innovation that was not originally chartered. For example, if quantum computing emerges as the next logical innovation to invest in—but the consortium charter does not explicitly state that it will make an investment in this particular technology, then this consortium would miss out on investing in the next big thing. These rules often stress fairness among members and emphasize values-based policies such as equal voting rights and unanimous consent requirements. However, the rigidity of this approach hampers the ability to think outside of the box.

In a joint venture model, flat organizational structures and empowered teams ensure innovation is sparked through creativity and design thinking approaches. Teams are given more latitude to explore, fail fast, and take initiative.

SHIFT FROM COST CENTERS TO PROFIT CENTER

Consortia are often structured as cost centers and achieve amazing cost savings in the first three to five years. Unfortunately, cost center structures emphasize efficiency, not growth. They lack funding mechanisms to support investments for long-term growth. Often the savings that materialized are paid out to members and not reinvested into the DDDN.

To succeed, a joint venture model should be designed as a profit center focused on sustainable growth and profitability. The goal should be to build growth businesses and generate profitable revenue by adopting a long-term mindset. With adequate funding and a profit center structure, joint venture startups can more easily focus on the commercialization of ideas. They can focus on selling, growing, and building partnerships as they invest profits to grow the business instead of making payouts to members. The profit center model gives license to focus on the Rule of 40 and grow.

SHIFT FROM A PROFITABLE-SHARED SERVICES EXIT TO AN IPO

Achieving scale and profitability drives the mission of most consortia. Yet in a business landscape where return on capital requires a larger exit strategy, consortia appear to be a drain on resources instead of creating new value for members.

In a joint venture model, members should work toward an IPO-type of event as an attractive exit strategy and to create the right motivation for each member to invest (and maintain their level of investment consistent) in the venture. The end game should be to create a new self-sufficient, independent entity that in the future grows to be even bigger than the venture membership and can stand up as a competitor to future digital giants that might be built via other partnerships.

While forming a joint venture to create a DDDN requires less financial investment than starting one on one's own, it does require more orchestration among the members and a bigger investment of time by each of them. Avoiding the pitfalls that typically lead to consortia failing and instead adopting these best practices will ensure a higher likelihood that the DDDN can be successfully created via a joint venture model. When they do, these joint venture startup models set the stage to challenge existing digital giants.

Three Models to Galvanize Joint Venture Startups

Bringing together partners for joint venture startups is not easy. Along with a solid business model and adherence to the best practices described above, joint ventures require a higher calling, a mission and purpose with an uber theme. There are three common powerful "callings" that bring these unique partnerships together: a common enemy, the creation of a network of networks, and a commonwealth of self-interest.

COMMON BUSINESS MODEL ENEMY DRIVEN BY A CLOUD VENDOR

A good reason to form a joint venture is to defeat a common enemy. Individually, each partner in the venture might not be able to go up against an existing digital giant because it doesn't have the resources to create a DDDN, or doesn't have a big enough network or content or offerings. By pooling resources, several organizations whose businesses are threatened by the same digital giant can mount a counterattack.

A hypothetical example of a joint venture created to battle a common business model enemy would be a cloud vendor-led, anti-Amazon alliance of consumer good brands and retailers. DDDNs need access to exponential technologies that can process massive amounts of data, automate processes, and apply tools such as artificial intelligence to identify signal intelligence. The ability to bring a large corpus of data, massive computing power, rapid deployments, and awesome math talent allows cloud vendors to play a key role in creating joint venture startups.

The goal of this hypothetical consumer good joint venture would be to align content (manufacturers of consumer goods and retailers) and network (delivery companies, distributors, and retailers) partners to join forces. The cloud vendor might start by inviting a few brands like Kimberly-Clark, Procter & Gamble, and Unilever to join the venture as "content members"—their involvement would guarantee enough content to populate a new DDDN. The venture might also bring in retailers such as Metro, Target, or Walmart to provide content. Adding one or two delivery companies such as DHL, FedEx, or UPS to the venture as "network members" would allow the venture to scale.

The cloud vendor's initial $50 to $100 million investment would provide the seed funds. Each network and content member's $5 million investment would fund the venture using capital, not operating budget. The capital investment could bring from $200 million to $500 million to the initial funding round, enabling the joint venture an eighteen- to twenty-four-month period to establish a minimum viable offering without short-term constraints.

To establish this minimum viable offering, the cloud vendor would bring existing software development assets to bear much faster. Leveraging the existing supply chain, commerce, customer experience, and retail capabilities that members bring to the table would allow the joint venture to benefit from immediate expertise and create a minimum viable offering quickly. Having the tech vendor as the lead can create exponential economies of scale. The goal of this venture from day one will be to take market share and win over key customer/partners from Amazon.

The joint venture will achieve monetization value not from transactional efficiencies, but from the insights the DDDN will be able to collect and analyze which will power the future of the venture. By having domain expertise and plenty of demand signals to make contextual decisions, the joint venture will be able to identify future offerings, gauge customer sentiment, determine optimal supply chains, and enable new business models.

The joint venture would also provide a vehicle to aggregate resources from all the members to increase their total investment percentage. Amazon reinvests up to 10 percent of its profits into innovation and growth, much more than the average brand and retailer. But if each member pledges 0.5 percent of its budget, in aggregate the venture could potentially invest more R&D than Amazon, their biggest competitor. Any innovations created by the new joint venture would be shared by the members, which will gain from a community focused on creating IP for the purpose of beating Amazon and improving their viability.

Designed as an A/B voting share structure, the cloud company would receive Class A shares which hold 10 votes per share, while the rest of the joint venture partners would be issued Class B shares (1 vote per share). With 1 million Class A shares issued and 5 million Class B shares, the cloud company could serve as a benevolent dictator. Joint venture members would participate with this explicit understanding but also have the ability to veto significant issues such as change of control, investment costs above a certain threshold, and other decisions requiring a supermajority of membership. With a benevolent dictatorship model, the team would have the flexibility and authority to move fast. Given the pace of innovation by Amazon, this joint venture would have to build agile business models and break traditional rules fast in order to catch up.

Once established as a separate and independent entity—and viable competitor to Amazon—the joint venture would have an opportunity to fully spin it out. An IPO exit would not only attract top talent to the venture and keep teams focused, it would also provide a meaningful outcome for all members.

NETWORK OF NETWORKS MODEL DRIVEN BY AN IT SERVICES PROVIDER

Another model that bring organizations together to form a joint venture is the desire to create a "network of networks," that is, a group of interconnected networks that share resources. Unlike the common enemy approach, this model focuses on building out the multi-sided network economies by value chain, customer segment, or geography. IT services providers can play a key role as the exponential technology enabler and orchestrator of value chains in this joint venture model.

An example of this model is an IT services provider that brings a coalition of companies with large facilities footprints—think big retailers like Walmart or Home Depot, large food franchises like McDonald's, big data center like Equinix, and commercial real estate services firms like CB Richard Ellis or Jones Lang La-Salle—together with smart building networks—Philips Lighting, Siemens, Schneider Electric, Johnson Control, Thyssenkrupp, Honeywell, and United Technologies to provide proactive monitoring, field service, operational efficiency, and personalization for building operators.

The IT service would put up $25 million in seed funds. Each member of the coalition would invest $5 million from their capital (not operating) budgets, bringing from $50 million to $100 million to the initial funding round. Players outside of the network would feel compelled to join and invest at the formation stage or face threats of going out of business. Potential joint venture partners across the value chain would be placed in fear of missing out (FOMO) mode.

The IT services provider through the joint venture would accelerate the delivery of a smart building coalition by creating and setting standards required for faster adoption across the network. Standardization would provide a foundation for enabling faster growth and innovation. Using its expertise in large system implementation and projects, the IT services provider would rapidly determine the minimum viable offerings along with each iteration required for success. Its infrastructure experience would enable rapid integration. Its experience in business processing outsourcing would provide the remote monitoring and process scale. Its applications experience would improve orchestration of the final offering.

Like the "common enemy" model, the joint venture would have a benevolent dictatorship governance structure, led by the IT services provider, giving it the agility to make decisions fast and respond to market needs. The IT services provider would deliver on transparent and agreed-upon road maps. Any IP created for the purpose of creating smart-building offerings would be shared by the joint venture members. Like the "common enemy" model, from day one the end goal of the venture would be to move toward an IPO exit to deliver a big payoff to all venture members.

COMMONWEALTH OF SELF-INTEREST DRIVEN BY AN INDUSTRY ASSOCIATION

In the commonwealth of self-interest, organizations with a similar business model or monetization models that do not directly compete make a strategic decision to create a win-win partnership. In some cases, the commonwealth of self-interest, as popularized by the godfather of CRM, Paul Greenberg, brings together head-on competitors who see a benefit in creating industry standards or reducing redundancy.[1] As we talked about in Chapter 4, a large opportunity awaits to create new business models based on airline mileage programs and cryptocurrency. This approach can be led at the industry association level, not the actual airline, hotel, or cruise line.

A hypothetical example of such a joint venture model is one of the two main travel industry associations, either IATA or SITA, playing a role in bringing together the world's first travel-oriented cryptocurrency system built from industry players' loyalty programs. One of these leading associations, could partner with global airline alliances such as the Star Alliance, One World, and SkyTeam and with hotel groups like Marriott, Hilton, and Intercontinental Hotel Group to take a cross-border, tax free, cryptocurrency to market. The opportunity to standardize funding models, loyalty programs, and the creation of cross-border commerce at a global scale of potentially 3 billion members would easily bring a commonwealth of self-interest together.

Using an A/B voting share structure, the association would

create a new joint venture startup and receive ten votes for every Class A share versus Class B shares. Each airline and hotel group would be investors, and pledge the existing cash value of their loyalty programs as an asset value in this new venture. The industry association could also raise additional outside funds if necessary.

The existing alliances between airlines and between airlines and hotel groups have already eased the complexity of sharing data across multiple systems. The advent of cryptocurrency based on loyalty programs points enables new markets to be created where points are earned at $0.01 a mile and often redeemed at more than $0.02 a mile. The built-in profit margin on the loyalty program exchange rate ensures profitability on day one. With all the players involved, this travel industry joint venture could go after the financial services firms that have had a lock on airlines via credit card programs by taking over the payments aspect and reducing the transaction fees paid to credit card issuers.

The collaboration skills that the existing global alliances have honed working together in the past, as well as their industry specific capabilities, could enable a rapid prototype to be delivered. The creation of this cryptocurrency would also spawn new partnerships with retailers, financial services, digital services companies, and ad networks. By removing the complexity of each travel partner creating their own cryptocurrency, joint venture partners would gain the time and resources to build out new product offerings instead of experimenting with their own cryptocurrency projects.

The travel industry already benefits from the global distribution system or GDS (a computerized network that allows companies access to realtime inventory of airline seats and hotel rooms), which plays a key role in helping them understand customer demand and needs. The creation of this cryptocurrency will expand the venture partner's opportunities into adjacent commerce areas such as payments, smart contracts, and personalization. Members will finally have their key information in their hands and be able to create new customized offerings based on customer demand such as personalized offers, improved search targeting, and better input on custom vacations.

In this model, this association-driven joint venture would be a future IPO event. As customers and partners, venture members could exit the investment and cash out but remain as partners. This capital allocation would be seen as both a long-term opportunistic investment and defensive play.

Competing Against Built-from-the-Ground-Up Digital Giants

While it may not seem easy at first, partnering to create and orchestrate a digital giant is less challenging than going head-on against a built-from-the-ground-up digital giant. Even with the joint venture startup models, competing against these digital giants should never ever be underestimated. Compared to joint ventures, in the fight for market share, profits, and customer mindshare, built-from-the-ground-up digital giants often respond faster, adapt more quickly to battlefield conditions, and go to market faster with new innovations—all while designing new barriers to entry.

Joint venture startups must find ways to match the decision velocity of built-from-the-ground-up digital giants who often have founder leaders with a long-term mindset and a power dynamic of super-voting and dual class share ownership structures. Simply put, built-from-the-ground-up digital giants can make decisions much more quickly, even if they are public companies. To counter a built-from-the-ground-up digital giant's ability to adapt and move quickly requires the joint venture to invest in agile governance models and dynamic leadership.

But joint venture startups do have a significant advantage. They have the added benefit of a larger and more diverse board membership and value chain ecosystem that can provide a diversity of thought. And more important, they've built the memory muscle when it comes to crafting win-win alliances and infusing a "partner first" strategy into the DNA of the organization.

Inside the IBM Food Trust Partnership

IBM is a pioneer of leading joint ventures successfully. Their IBM Food Trust is an excellent example of how to apply the best practices described in this chapter to build a successful joint venture.

In 2016, IBM set off to create a blockchain network for a smarter, more sustainable, and safer ecosystem of growers, food manufacturers, wholesalers and distributors, food logistics companies, food retailers, food service providers, and other food-related organizations. It has over two hundred clients including big brands such as Walmart, Nestle, Tysons Foods, Carrefour, Albertsons, and others. IBM handles over 20 million transactions on 17,000 products with 750,000 traces conducted as of 2019.[2]

IBM's approach is unique in the food industry and unique among IBM's partnerships. IBM's joint venture approach applies six out of the eleven best practices detailed earlier in the chapter:

- **Engender motivation to create a safer and more secure food supply chain.** IBM has brought together a joint venture startup to enable the entire food supply chain to come together. The partners are committed to ensuring food safety, transparent supply chains, and provenance of data.

- **Emphasize growth and innovation.** The offerings provided by IBM Food Trust focus on innovations in cost savings and regulatory compliance, while enabling growth through hyper-trust. When a network member trusts a participant, their transactions are more quickly approved, default rates on payments go down, and orders are delivered on time. Customers are willing to pay a premium to be able to trace the provenance of food from its source to consumption. Customers want to know that their sashimi or medicine was kept at the proper temperature and they will be happy to pay to know their honey or extra virgin olive oil is truly pure.

- **Deliver minimum viable offering based on blockchain networks.** The IBM Food Trust Data Platform enables smart contracts that reduce the cost of manual paperwork and ensure compliance as two or more parties agree to predefined rules to track discrepancies. It also enables application programming interfaces (APIs), or how systems integrate and talk to each other, that process data on food traceability and other insights.[3] The first iteration focused on efficiencies in contracts. Future iterations have provided advanced capabilities on tracing. The product continues to grow in capability as the network grows.

- **Achieve monetization value from insight and AI.** The underlying blockchain capabilities provide hypertrust insights such as inventory visibility, shelf-life updates, dwell time optimization, and cold chain management. The value of the network is in these insights which provide data on supplier reliability and food provenance.

- **Encourage new IP and innovation.** The IBM Food Trust created an advisory council composed of certification bodies, regulators and standards, and consumers that provide input to the IBM team so they can prioritize what resources to develop and what new capabilities ought to be designed.

Across the food supply chain, growers, food manufacturers, wholesalers, distributors, food logistics, food retailers, and food service share best practices that work their way back in to the offering.

- **Shift from rigid to agile organizational structures.** The input from member organizations guide the pace and depth of innovation of the network services. This input generates a constant stream of ideas that can be operationalized. Designing for agility enables a more responsive IBM team to address network partner requests.

As a pioneer in these joint venture startup models, IBM can apply the other best practices in the future. In order to shift from a highly deliberative federation of consensus to a more streamlined and action-oriented benevolent dictator, IBM could raise a venture fund to run and operate its joint venture startup. In the shift from cost center to profit center, the joint venture startup would be set up for spin out and profitability. Future joint venture startups should be designed with an IPO exit strategy from its inception, so that an independent entity can be created.

Create a Culture of Abundance

The art of the joint venture startup requires a partnership strategy focused on a culture of abundance versus a culture of scarcity. In the old-world model, a culture of scarcity encourages individuals to compete for attention, safety, funding, staff time, resources, and space. Every win for one party is a loss for another. While everyone is acting in their own self-interest, there is no common purpose or shared goal. In fact, this approach is massively destructive to value chains and ecosystems. This win-lose culture creates a self-reinforcing mechanism of destruction and negative competition. Put simply, the culture of scarcity focuses on dividing the pie.

In a culture of abundance, participants in a joint venture still represent their self-interest but the shift to shared goals expands the pie for everyone—and empowers participants to make more pies while increasing demand for pies. With a mindset of abundance, joint ventures can focus on the value each partner brings to the table. When you carefully curate partners across the value chain you are able to bring a productive ecosystem together. If a participant isn't able to bring explicit value that can be quantified, then the participant should not be invited into the joint venture. This is crucial to cultivating a culture of abundance that fosters the mutual respect and trust required for every joint venture startup to successfully battle other digital giants.

8

WHERE DO WE GO FROM HERE?

The internet celebrated its fiftieth birthday in October 2019. In half a century, it spawned massive adoption of new technologies and business models and led to big improvements in our society from increased connectivity and commerce to decentralized access, democratized computing, and a new age of information sharing. The internet has also enabled the development of other foundational technologies of the digital age such as mobile phones, cloud computing, 5G, big data, the Internet of Things, and AI. These, in turn, unleashed a wave of innovation and creativity the world has never seen before. The unprecedented technology adoption, access to capital, and openness to new business models has led to the rise of the digital giants and the DDDNs that we've discussed in this book.

But perhaps most astonishing is the speed in which digital giants have grown and inserted themselves into almost every aspect of our lives. When 50 million users adopt a technology, experts consider it mainstream—it has achieved mass adoption. Technology adoption along with new business models used to take years. For example, it took seventy-five years for the telephone to reach 50 million users. But it only took Facebook Live twenty-four hours (see Figure 8.1.). Not only is the pace of change rapid, but also is the pace of adoption and disintermediation of existing business models.

TELEPHONE	INTERNET	INSTAGRAM	ANGRY BIRDS
75 years	4 years	19 months	35 days
RADIO	FACEBOOK	YOUTUBE	POKÉMON GO
38 years	2 years	10 months	19 days
TELEVISION	SMART SPEAKERS	TWITTER	FACEBOOK LIVE
13 years	22 months	9 months	24 hours

FIGURE 8.1. SPEED OF ADOPTION OF NEW TECHNOLOGIES OVER THE YEARS.

Fifty years later, the basic promises of the internet—that it would democratize access, increase the speed of innovation, and lead to exponential improvements in efficiency—have come to pass. Digital giants have played a big role in making them possible. We carry more computing power in our pocket than was used to put a man on the moon. We can work from anywhere and have the ability to move information at the speed of light. We are more connected to others than ever, as these technologies can bring the world together with improved communications and shared experiences.

While the new world of digital giants brings even more promise for the future, I must be honest: I am scared about the age of duopolies. The rise of digital giants is happening at lightning speed and the duopolies that will emerge in the near future will unleash an uncontrollable wrath of power. I'm scared to enter an era in which every digital giant wants to rule the world and where each successive wave of technology enables more control by fewer and fewer entities. For example, the promise of the internet has been about democratized access and open markets. Digital giants strive to get everyone connected—fulfilling the basic promise of the internet that everyone should have access to information. But to what end? Yes, we are better at sharing information across the globe than ever before, yet we have more division, and more political and social unrest.

In the Chinese Communist Party's China, members of the government have used digital giants to silence free speech. Users of Tencent's WeChat have seen the power of censorship on topics such as the Communist Party and even COVID-19. Even in the United States, an eagerness for political correctness and social mobs have limited speech on digital giants' platforms. These same digital giants have shown bias when defining free speech. We may be able to order anything we want, whenever we want— but are we truly happier? Are we more content? Do we have our freedoms and rights such as the ability to share our opinions freely, the right to our privacy, or the right to retain our personal data if digital giants apply their values on society? The fact that we have entrusted so much power to the digital giants without limiting their controls will affect how we communicate, what we can say, how we can think, and the perception of right or wrong. To entrust this much power without the appropriate checks and balances invites totalitarian control by private entities.

If we don't invest the time to understand how the age of duopolies will change our political, social, and business landscape, we will not be able to take action to preserve humanity, personal freedoms, and our privacy. We need to learn how to create the right equilibrium between the pace of innovation, free market competition, profit, and personal freedoms and rights.

To move forward, we need to first understand what lies ahead. As with all disruptions, we'll see a spectrum of change. The life cycle of digital giants will go through four phases: the dawn of digital giants, the age of digital giants, the decline of digital giants, and the dusk of digital giants. In this chapter, I'll apply a classic PESTEL analysis to each of these phases. This analysis will help us uncover how these digital giants will impact politics (P), economics (E), society (S), technology (T), environment (E), and legislation (L). This PESTEL analysis, I hope, will help organizations, policymakers, business leaders, and individuals understand what factors to consider in scenario planning for the next decade.

The Dawn of Digital Giants: Rush to Create Digital Giants

We are currently in the dawn of digital duopolies and the mad rush to create the next hundred digital giants in fifty markets that will consume the world's resources in capital, talent, and energy. As I described in this book, there are abundant opportunities to build DDDNs from scratch or by partnering with others. Those organizations that don't do either will experience deep declines in value. The accelerated collapse of industries into value chains, the increased popularity of vertically integrated digital monetization models, and competition among nation states for dominance will forever transform markets into a handful of winner-takes-all duopolies.

As we look into the future, here's what we can expect on the six macro-environmental factors:

POLITICAL

Domestically, politicians will pretend to bash on digital giants to appear to be taking a "tough" stance on tech when convenient during election cycles, while happily taking their campaign contributions and receiving their lobbyists. Globally, the ownership of critical infrastructure, the building blocks and tools needed to create a digital giant, will remain in private hands. These building blocks include how a DDDN is created, access to the internet, affordable computing power and storage, tools to author content or code, cybersecurity technology, payment technologies, artificial intelligence, and other core capabilities.

However, some nation states are using their digital giants as proxies in a war for global digital dominance. A good example is TikTok, which in 2020 was accused of collecting American citizens' privacy data on behalf of the Chinese government. Those nation states who have not developed policies to spur digital giants are mostly content with the public good and innovations being provided at minimal financial cost. Who doesn't like a free social network or no cost email?

The BeiDou Navigation Satellite System (BDS-3), China's global navigation system known as their "North Star," is a GPS system with thirty-five global positioning satellites in orbit.[1] It is also a good example of how nation states will step in to develop critical infrastructure to build data supremacy and create a dual-use system for commercial and national security purposes. GPS is a foundational technology used in military applications, autonomous vehicles, geophysical exploration, and surveillance. As part of China's larger Belt and Road initiative, BDS-3 is a foreign policy and economic trade project to build critical infrastructure in seventy countries to exert more economic and political influence in the region. Instead, these critical capabilities may come at an extreme cost to those countries that accept them or in some cases to those that do not accept them. The Chinese government expects those who want to use their GPS network to conform to or publicly avow their support for China's foreign policy and economic goals. They may demand that countries in the GPS network use the system in order to be "protected" by the Chinese Community Party's military. Using critical infrastructure as coercion for policy is part of their plan.

Consequently, nation states like China will give their country's digital giants a leg up by making large critical infrastructure investments. These investments will bring together academia, military, and startups to create state-influenced and state-owned partnerships. China, for example, has already invested trillions in artificial intelligence, quantum computing, internet companies, social networks, chip design, and offensive capabilities in cyber war. It uses these innovations to supply other autocratic regimes with key digital technologies as part of their foreign and economic policy strategy. This model, where the nation state serves as a digital giant and an enabler of other digital giants, will be replicated by other autocratic regimes and consortia of smaller nations who have not yet created economies of scale.

ECONOMIC

Digital giants will rapidly grow in terms of market share and profit growth. This concentration of stock market cap growth will exacerbate the digital divide between those companies that have a DDDN and those that don't. We already see this in the 2020s with 20 percent of the S&P's value comprising five stocks: Apple, Microsoft, Amazon, Google, and Facebook.[2] Distinct winners and losers will emerge. Where others fail, the digital giants will step in and transform their business models, creating a plethora of digital monetization models. The competition for dominance has already resulted in a handful of $1 trillion market cap companies that represent the earliest winners of the dawn of digital giants: Google, Amazon, Microsoft, and Apple (the GAMA group).

SOCIETAL

As digital giants infiltrate every aspect of life, most of society will continue to embrace the convenience that they bring and, therefore, support the breakneck pace of innovation that comes with them. New business models provide benefits to early adopters from improving how food is ordered and delivered to how health care is provided. The consumerization of industries will lead to the greatest creation of contextual data the world will have seen, feeding every digital giant's signal intelligence apparatus.

TECHNOLOGY

Digital giants will fund the greatest amount of technology innovation the world has seen. Their collective financial investment of hundreds of billions of dollars will lead to tremendous breakthroughs in exponential technologies such as autonomous vehicles, new visualization technologies such as mixed reality, brain wave systems that allow you to control interfaces with your thoughts, advances of biology in a digital world, and space exploration. Digital giants have already placed their bets in these technologies to transform industries and dominate value chains.

ENVIRONMENTAL

A rallying cry for green initiatives will emerge as digital giants weave efficiency into their "social good stories." As they build huge data centers to power their DDDNs, there will be a focus on energy efficient designs. These digital giants will consume almost 50 percent of the world's computing resources. Subsequently, large cloud data centers will improve their power efficiency. Meanwhile, consumption of power will improve with better power management and new battery technologies built on organic chemistry. Expect a more judicious use of rare earth materials, which are critical to chip design. The proliferation of digital giants will accelerate efforts to deliver "a circular economy," characterized by zero waste production and the continual use of materials and resources.

LEGISLATIVE

Regulatory environments will remain laissez-faire in countries with pro-digital giant policies. Data privacy and privacy rights legislation will favor digital giants as they continue to disrupt existing industries. Even as they amass a large concentration of power in markets, any push to regulate them will be countered with arguments on the benefits that they and their innovations bring to society. Moreover the large number of people that work for digital giants in key voting areas will quell a lot of cries for regulation (e.g., Amazon's 800,000 employees, Microsoft's 156,000, Apple's 135,000, and Google's 119,000).

THE LEADING INDICATOR OF THE RISE OF DIGITAL GIANTS: COLLAPSED INDUSTRIES ALONG NEW VALUE CHAINS

The rapid collapse of industries along new value chains will be the most critical sign that the rise of digital giants is accelerating. Two examples of this collapse can be seen in Tesla and Apple.

While many see Tesla as an auto manufacturer—and some even see them as a clean energy pioneer—Elon Musk's ambition is to create a digital giant. In fact, Tesla already is one, disguised as a transportation and energy company. At its core, every Tesla vehicle is a data collection agent. With it, Tesla captures information about driver behavior, location via its GPS system and cameras, and energy use and consumption. When Tesla, which has already made inroads with autonomous driving, achieves full self-driving or FSD capabilities sometime in 2023, it will have almost 2 million vehicles on the road. With all the data it will be able to collect, the company will be in a position to go after various markets.

Autonomous vehicles not in use by their owners could be put

into ride-hailing scenarios, deliver meals and goods, and identify the top destinations and traffic jams inside a city. Tesla's Semi, an all-electric Class 8 heavy-duty truck that can travel five hundred miles on a single charge, was designed to create autonomous transportation fleets.[3] Since these trucks won't require a driver that needs rest, there will be fewer limitations to how far the truck can travel in a day. Using its own underwriting data, Tesla will be able to self-insure their fleet and offer insurance to customers who are willing to provide their driving data. In addition, as it accumulates experience in the insurance business, Tesla will be able to improve vehicle design by studying loss data to develop easier-to-repair parts. With the acquisition of SolarCity, the global solar panel installer, Tesla is also sitting at the forefront of transit electrification and decentralized power grid management. The company can use the Tesla Power Wall, a battery storage unit, to bring solar power into a house and back into the grid. In essence, they can generate power, distribute power, and efficiently consume power.

These new business and monetization models would allow Tesla to collapse industries along new value chains built on data from location-based services, insurance, and power generation.

As digital giants collapse industries along value chains, they will also expand their business models to deploy new digital monetization techniques. Apple is a prime example. For years, Apple's heavy reliance on revenues from sales of its hardware, especially iPhones, was seen as a mixed blessing. Investors and stock analysts would focus on forecasting the unit volumes of Apple's products in order to determine the economic health of the smartphone industry. However, Apple's growth of its service revenues from a single digit percentage of the company's overall revenues to almost a quarter of total revenues since 2019 demonstrates how services monetization can expand total addressable market.[4] This shift from relying on revenue from devices to expanding the full value of every device has created almost a 500 percent revenue growth from ApplePay, Apple's own credit cards, the AppleTV+ subscription streaming service, the subscription gaming service Apple Arcade, and Apple Care warranty protection.[5] The result has been the creation of a $1 trillion market cap company on its way to exceed $100 billion in quarterly revenues and cross the $2 trillion market cap milestone.

The Age of Digital Giants: Fierce Competition for Digital Dominance

The continuing collapse of industries along new value chains will continue and the Fortune 500 and Global 2000 will face an accelerated decimation. One hundred digital giants in fifty markets will emerge to play a dominant role across the globe, leading to a battle between two players in each market by geography, value chain, and networked economy. During this period, digital giants will have massively automated key business processes and mined their data to create artificial intelligence capabilities that will set off the DDDN flywheel. Automation and the reduced use of physical inputs will produce extreme efficiency that will, in turn, lead to the reduction of millions of jobs. This level of extreme efficiency will reduce overall consumption, creating an economic depression in many markets as the number of goods and services needed will be rationalized and the available number of buyers will drop. Considering a reduction in overall global population, markets will contract and the world will enter a global recession. The good news, improvements in environment and sustainability will grow exponentially. As digital giants rush to control computing power costs, they will improve the energy efficiency of their operations and prompt investments in more efficient and renewable sources of electricity.

As the digital giants battle out in duopolies, they—and

governments—will come to the conclusion that monopolies are the best model for commoditizing critical infrastructure and services. Digital giants will make the case for mergers and acquisition to meet their efficiency targets. Shareholders seeking growth will fall in line and the push for cost savings and efficiencies will continue the endless cycle of job losses and efficiency cuts. Governments will align with the need to dismantle the digital giants but will be powerless as monopolies will threaten to cut off services if challenged.

The age of digital giants will impact the six macro-environmental factors in the following way:

POLITICAL

Digital giants will continue to take ownership of critical infrastructure such as payments, connectivity, and means of content production and distribution. In fact, as most value chains will be controlled by no more than two players, this high concentration of critical infrastructure in private hands will start to concern people. The lack of government oversight and inability of the public sector to craft policies that rein in the power of the digital giants will lead to massive societal and an eventual political backlash. The rapid ascent of digital giants into duopoly markets while smaller players fail to gain traction, overall competition is held at bay, prices increase, and innovation slows will lead to mounting calls for anti-trust provisions.

ECONOMIC

Digital giants will dominate most of the valuation in the global stock markets, their sum total representing more than half of the valuation of the S&P 500. In this phase, one winner in every collapsed value chain will have emerged and investors will flock to these winners at all costs, making heavy bets on a handful of companies. The remaining players will battle for the number 2 and number 3 spots by market share, revenues, data amassed, and profit per employee. At this point, there will be no doubt that digital giants will have crushed the competition and potentially stifled future growth.

SOCIETAL

In the age of duopolies, companies will compete for our personal data. Digital giants will compensate us for our data—from location, to transactions, to social networks data—with access to goods and services. Those who want to live off the grid or do not want to share their data will have to pay a premium for not giving up the data that power digital giants' DDDNs. Activists for universal basic income will ask digital giants to fund this initiative by paying customers for their personal data via a one-time use, period subscription, or lifetime. This battle for personal data and the normalization of surveillance capitalism, where personal data is commoditized for the purpose of profits, will emerge as one of the biggest societal issues during the age of duopolies.

TECHNOLOGY

The massive data collection efforts of digital giants will lead to the early development of a general artificial intelligence. This general AI system will have the ability to develop early sentient and autonomous capabilities that will humanize machines. Meanwhile advances in human application programming interfaces (APIs) will take the human computer paradigm to new levels as machines mimic humans. This convergence toward the singularity—the idea, made popular by futurist Ray Kurzweil, that exponential increases in technologies will lead to a superintelligence that rivals that of humans—will begin in the age of digital giants.

ENVIRONMENTAL

Overall efficiencies from significant adoption of AI will help lower carbon emissions, optimize transportation systems, minimize redundancy in processes, reduce paper waste, and efficiently allocate resources through highly precise optimization algorithms. New technologies that use bio-based fuels and power cells will create both sustainable and renewable sources of power as digital giants race to drive down the cost of energy for their computing power. Hence, computing power per kilowatts per hour will be increased by a factor of ten as energy costs drop by another factor of ten. In general, digital giants will understand that environmental sustainability and their corporate survival and success are intertwined.

LEGISLATIVE

Legislative bodies will use privacy issues as a foil to tax digital giants in an attempt to control their dominance. As societal attitudes shift from laissez-faire involvement to active protests, a battle for data rights will emerge. Regulatory agencies will start deliberating and debating how digital giants provide fair and equitable market access to their DDDNs.

How Industries Will Collapse Along Data Value Chains

Companies tend to compete in industries. Even multinational conglomerates think in industries. However, companies need to anticipate the convergence toward vertically integrated value chains and the competition for data across value chains and networks. Two examples of emerging data value chains where digital giants will build, acquire, and consolidate over time are the areas of where and what we eat, and of how we access healthcare.

The food supply chain—from food production, distribution, retailers and grocers, to restaurants and food delivery—is quite complex. The family farms and large agribusinesses that supply your food like mushrooms and meat often rely on large restaurant chains, entertainment venues like movie theaters and stadiums, and institutional food services at schools, office campuses, hospitals, and more for most of their revenue. During the pandemic, the demand shifted from large institutional buyers to individuals. Caught flat-footed, the various players in the food supply chain could not deliver their goods cost effectively at scale to individual consumers. On one hand, grocery chains such as Aldi, Carrefour, Costco, Walmart, Whole Foods, and others faced supply chain disruptions. On the other hand, food delivery companies like Postmates, Just Eat, Swiggy, and Grubhub saw an increase in business but have had to battle the ride hailing services Gojek, Oola, and Uber Eats while simultaneously disrupting traditional players such as Domino's Pizza on last mile delivery.

While the battle between individual players in the food chain seems obvious, the market is ripe for disruption. A competitor or new entity will come in and collapse the entire value chain with an integrated strategy across food production, distribution, retailers and grocers, to restaurants and food delivery. In the world of digital giants, you follow the data, not just the money. Given the current devastated food service supply chain that includes farmers, cold supply chains, wholesalers, and restaurant supply companies, the data pipeline on supply chains, demand chains, customer preferences, route data, and weather will converge to create a new digital giant around last mile food delivery. The shared data will provide plenty of demand signals, pricing information, and supplier reliability information.

Meanwhile, as we discussed in Chapter 1, ghost kitchens will emerge as another value chain disruptor. These ghost kitchens are massive facilities that offer dozens of branded "restaurants"—from a salad factory to a burger joint, a Thai bistro, a Korean BBQ, California organic, Chinese takeout, fine Italian—in one location. The market once dominated by a handful of mom and pop restaurants will emerge as a vertically integrated digital giant that goes from farm to table. How? Ghost kitchens and food delivery networks will converge to take on the full vertically integrated offering. As they gain traction, they will invest their profits into acquiring farms, food producing companies, cold supply chain players, restaurant supply companies, and distribution networks. Thus, the battle begins with the edge—food delivery apps—but a consolidation of key resources in farm land, warehouse space for cooking, and autonomous delivery will create a barrier to entry to competitors, as they will not have access to the food producers or the customers. Without them, investors will not fund them.

Today's health system is a patchwork mess at best and a chaotic bureaucratic ball of regulatory morass at worst. Very little focus has been made on preventative care as a means to reduce overall healthcare expenses. In fact, a 2017 report from the U.S. Department of Health and Human Services showed that the twenty most expensive conditions make up 43.3 percent of all hospital stays and the majority of the conditions that lead to them come from acute health issues that could be addressed with a preventative approach.[6] The potential disruption of preventative care sits at the intersection of how patient data is shared and utilized to improve outcomes. To successfully bring patient data together, healthcare will bring about a collapse of industries from insurance, pharmaceutical companies, healthcare providers, consumer electronics, and digital giants.

Every pharmaceutical company wants de-identified records to complete their prospective trials and bring their drugs to market. Enrolling patients for clinical trials and securing their patient records is a big business, an estimated $100 billion by 2030. This battle for patient data is only increasing as the stakes to get a drug from molecule to market have grown bigger: Today it takes a decade and almost $1 billion to do so.

Digital giants, sensing an opportunity to bring together a DDDN that captures this precious patient health information, are clamoring to build out their stake in healthcare. For example, Apple has already jumped into the market with Apple Research-Kit and CareKit, both part of HealthKit, which allow developers to create apps that make enrolling patients into studies and patient record sharing easier.[7] Apple has the trust of consumers to emerge as a healthtech company.

Meanwhile, Amazon's invested in its own healthcare system, Amazon Care, a telehealth service that provides medical consultation and prescription services online and offline, currently only available to its employees. Haven, a joint venture with Amazon, Berkshire Hathaway, and JPMorgan Chase created to benefit their employees, is trying to apply technology and AI to simplify the complex healthcare system and improve the health outcomes of their employees.[8] Amazon has also launched PillPack, a full-service pharmacy catering to people who take multiple medications. The service coordinates their prescriptions and refills to ensure they never run out, presorts their medications in individual packets according to when they should be taken, and delivers them for free.[9] Amazon has begun the acquisition and consolidation of the healthcare value chain around patient data.

Other digital giants have not sat still. Microsoft wants to dethrone Amazon as the key player in the health cloud with long-standing partnerships such as with the dominant electronic medical record (EMR) provider, Epic. It is has taken a stance as a partner to healthcare players, rather than as their competitor. Google agreed to acquire Fitbit for $2.1 billion in November 2019, and has invested in Verily, a separate subsidiary and research organization focused on the study of life sciences, which has been focusing on using AI to better healthcare.[10]

Expect future digital giants to create inroads into healthcare delivery with the goal of amassing patient data for research, delivery, and underwriting. They might first acquire an electronic medical record company such as Epic, Cerner, Care Cloud, Athenahealth, or Allscripts that would give them a head start with patient records as the core identifier. They could even acquire a health IT company like IQVIA which has amassed a trove of patient data used for clinical trials.

An acquisition or a partnership with a large insurer by any digital giant would also give that company the ability to mine vast amounts of data to identify the healthiest patients, lowest risk profiles, efficacy of drug testing, improved healthcare outcomes in the patient setting, operational efficiencies at healthcare providers, and preventative measures in healthcare capitation. Insurers have already consolidated by amassing polices outside of healthcare into property and casualty, auto, and life. As they continued to aggregate covered lives, these digital giants would know whom to insure with the lowest risk, understand which hospitals had the best outcomes, and determine which drug would have the best efficacy with which genetic profile.

The Decline of Digital Giants: Era of Distrust and Delusion

The decline of digital giants will start with an overwhelming backlash against them. The first fissures will seem to be a series of small backlashes with "fringe" groups unplugging from the digital economy. Radicals will band together to vandalize and destroy critical infrastructure used to collect data, suppress innovation, and grip economies. The combination of hacktivists, anti-trust sentiment, and the declining levels of innovation will have global governments questioning their support of digital giants.

The decline of digital giants will impact the six macro-environmental factors in the following way:

POLITICAL

Short of a revolution, those in power and with close ties and financial interests to digital giants will be forced to choose between the public good and these digital giants. This immense pressure from the public will results in serious hearings on the impact of digital giants. Elections will be won by candidates who vow to break up them up. The public, jaded and tired of all the talk and no action from the past, will rally around candidates who will advocate turning much of the critical infrastructure and data troves in the hands of digital giants into an open source public good.

Hactivists—people who use digital tools and techniques to disrupt companies, governments, and individuals—will activate movements to free countries and individuals from the tyranny of digital giants. They will attack and take over critical infrastructure owned by digital giants in areas such as utilities, mapping systems, data collection devices, payments, internet access, and media. Along with digital attacks, physical violence will erupt near data centers and the headquarters of the digital giants. Hactivists will attempt to blow up the world's data centers and cloud computing facilities in order to stop digital giants. The revolution in the streets will lead to a movement to a disconnected and analog society that values individual privacy and privacy rights over profit.

ECONOMIC

Stunted economic growth will arise as the digital giants fail to grow. Lack of innovation, massive unemployment from automation and market consolidation, and the inability to compete outside of a digital giant's network, will create a confluence of factors limiting economic growth. Winner-takes-all models will create massive efficiencies in the system, however the savings are not distributed back into the market. Digital giants will have squeezed out all the efficiencies and taken all the gains.

SOCIETAL

A full backlash to globalism will peak. Nationalism and anti-digital giant sentiment will be at its highest levels and the resulting policies will lead to national duopolies and monopolies. Emerging societal trends will favor an anti-surveillance state and customers will unplug from data collection schemes. A general distrust of digital giants will escalate from backlash to full revolt.

TECHNOLOGY

The pace of innovation and breakthroughs will have slowed. Technological progress will be mired in IP lawsuits as digital giants battle each other for their patent portfolios and fundamental technologies. Ecosystems built on the platforms of digital giants which were thriving earlier will now fail to gain investment dollars as the digital giants turn to in-house development and tuck-in acquisitions to bolster their tech capability. This drive to reduce costs will continue to create more insular technology.

ENVIRONMENTAL

One of the bright spots of this phase is that digital giants will continue to make investments in social responsibility initiatives to improve their brand image. These investments will help battle the public perception of the evil digital giant. Much of the environmental science developed by digital giants will provide a future foundation for ensuring public good.

LEGISLATIVE

The complex regulatory environment will make it impossible for startups to challenge digital giants and will reinforce the notion that only the biggest players can afford to play. Politicians will respond to popular calls to keep evil foreign digital giants out of their countries. This massive rise in nationalism will limit the growth of startups to mostly the geographies they already operate in. The extreme nature of how digital giants will have dominated the world will come to an end as serious anti-trust measures will enter the political fray. Other than the nation states who deploy their own digital giants, global governments will call for the dismantling of digital giants. However, given the massive economic and societal impact these digital giants have on all aspects of the economy and society, the complexity of breaking them up will keep these full-scale efforts from being successful.

The Dusk of Digital Giants: Returning Power to the People

After two decades of digital giants dominating the global stage, a global revolution and outcry will overthrow digital giants. Governments, civil society, and new institutions will ensure citizens will have the right to critical infrastructure as a public good.

Many of the duopolies will be converted to public utilities. The fuel behind the digital giants—personal data—will be recognized and protected as a global human right. The shift to a *Star Trek* economy," where society pursues knowledge, not money or greed, will be in full force.

The dusk of digital giants will impact the six macro-environmental factors in the following way:

POLITICAL

Politicians will take all necessary steps to ensure that critical infrastructure is in the control of public hands. Digital giants will be forced to hand over capabilities to public utilities amidst new anti-trust sentiment. Ownership of future critical infrastructure for a digital world will be in the stewardship of the public sector. The political climate will favor incentivizing the next level of innovative business models and exponential technologies.

ECONOMIC

The breakup of digital giants and the shift to utility models will free up capital and resources to start the next wave of innovation. Startups will once again thrive as they pursue new innovations built on unhindered, shared critical infrastructure. The stock market will see a plethora of IPOs as well as new growth companies. Brand-new potential winners will emerge as the next set of post-digital giants emerge.

SOCIETAL

The right to be disconnected will emerge as a popular way of life. While digital will be infused throughout all aspects of life, privacy will be cherished as a fundamental principle in society. A

growing cadre of analog options will be championed and supported across industries including banking, retail, travel and hospitality, and even the public sector. With individual rights
championed after years of oppression by digital giants and au-
thoritarian governments, a balance between common public
good and individual freedoms will create new opportunities for
inclusion and understanding. How? The individual's consent will
be the first principle in how data is utilized except for cases of
public good such as health and extreme security scenarios.

TECHNOLOGY

With critical infrastructure delivered as a public good or utility,
these open source capabilities will usher new opportunities for
innovation. A convergence of biosciences, chemistry, and computer science will lead to new sapient forms of life. The move to
the singularity will require us to revisit digital ethics since what
we recognize as human and machine will continue to blur the
meaning of life. Quantum computing will be mainstream and
bio batteries will be in full-scale production.

ENVIRONMENTAL

The environmental benefits from the data harvested by digital giants contributes to improving the global environment. Once proprietary data becomes a public good, the knowledge unlocked from
decades of artificial intelligence will spawn new innovations in energy efficiency, climate modeling, and sustainable development.

LEGISLATIVE

Sweeping reforms will include a streamlined process to meet future regulations. As the top minds work to reform the digital

giants, new models and policies will emerge to prevent future dominance by digital giants. With calls for anti-trust regulations and the breakup of most digital giants out of the way, the regulatory framework will be simplified for smaller players. The government will try to build an AI to anticipate future legislative requirements and identify when an emerging digital giant may be deploying anti-trust tactics.

How to Prevent the Dystopian Future

These four phases of the lifecycle of digital giants highlights how one futurist scenario may emerge should policymakers stay the course in how we treat today's emerging digital giants. While my role is to help you build the next set of digital giants so you can thrive in the coming age of duopolies, I hope future leaders pay attention to how digital giants can impact negatively our society if left unchecked.

While each of the phases will take shape in one way or another, policymakers, startup founders, investors, and informed citizens must consider how to find the right balance between the benefits that digital giants bring to society and their potential detrimental impact. They need to implement mechanisms to balance access to markets, means of digital production, and encourage innovation and scale in order to avoid a dystopian future. How future digital giants will evolve will depend on how quickly policymakers around the world can implement these three actions today:

1. SECURE THE CRITICAL INFRASTRUCTURE AND DIGITAL BUILDING BLOCKS FOR PUBLIC GOOD

Today's core exponential technologies that advance the public good include 5G and 6G telecommunications standards, chip design technology, artificial intelligence, quantum computing, CRISPR gene editing techniques, digital payments, cybersecurity, and many more. These technologies power critical infrastructure that enable markets to be created, innovations to be distributed and flourish, and opportunities to access and fulfill goods and services. Some of the digital building blocks of critical infrastructure include internet connectivity, social networks, digital marketplaces, cloud computing resources, cryptocurrencies, cybersecurity, compression technologies, AI algorithmic libraries, identity systems, computer visioning, brain wave interfaces, and other technologies used to create new innovations. One should view these technologies as the LEGO blocks necessary to grow a small business to a full one trillion dollar company.

While digital giants invest hundreds of billions in the development, commercialization, and modernization of critical infrastructure and digital building blocks, at some point these tired and declining digital giants emerge as their own worst enemy, their own barriers of entry to competition, especially if each critical infrastructure and digital building block is built on a DDDN. In fact, the digital giants face the innovator's dilemma, made famous by Clayton Christensen, where fear of disrupting themselves leads to paralysis that hinders innovation.[11]

The owner and operator of the DDDN, usually a digital giant, can easily vertically integrate and monetize their own DDDN in a way that benefits them. For example, the digital giant may keep a competitor out of a marketplace, charge more for a critical component, or discount a product below the competitor's cost. The temptation to squash competition is human nature. To prevent anti-competitive behavior from happening, policies must be created by legislators, monitored by regulators or third party agencies at an AI scale, and enforced by anti-trust officials whenever market conditions warrant.

The U.S. Cybersecurity and Infrastructure Security Agency (CISA) has identified sixteen critical infrastructure sectors that policymakers should consider as they pursue protections from anti-trust violations, foreign influence, and unfair market domination: the chemical sector; commercial facilities sector; communications sector; critical manufacturing sector; dams sector; defense industrial base sector; emergency services sector; energy sector; food and agriculture sector; financial services sector; government facilities sector; healthcare and public health sector; information technology sector; nuclear reactors, materials, and waste sector; transportation systems sector; water and wastewater systems sector.[12] As each of these sectors increasingly become private and digitized, they become susceptible to monetization by digital giants.

Drafting preventive polices to safeguard these sectors from a digital giant power grab should be the top priority. In some cases, when a critical infrastructure becomes commoditized, that market transitions and transforms into a highly regulated public utility or public monopoly or opens up for full-scale free market competition where all players jointly fund the core infrastructure. For example, in a decentralized power market, all players in the system pay one entity to handle the management and repair of—and reinvestment in—the transmission grid infrastructure. In highly concentrated markets, anti-trust efforts should be proactively pursued to ensure fair competition.

2. ADVOCATE THE GLOBAL RECOGNITION OF PERSONAL DATA AS A HUMAN RIGHT

Data is the foundation of every digital giant's business model. Social media interactions, location information, medical records, DNA information, purchase history, and other personal data used today by digital giants to power their business models are often taken for granted by those very same digital giants. How the data is used, where it is stored, who has access to it, how it is monetized, and how it is modified often remains a mystery to the user. When a service is "free," it means that you are paying for access to the service by willingly sharing data: You become the product.

To curtail the potential abuses of personal data by digital giants, we must advocate for personal data to be a property right, and for data privacy to be recognized and enforced as a human right. Today, we have land titles to protect real estate property and patents and trademarks to protect intellectual property. A similar approach should be applied to protect personal data. Once personal data becomes a property, every individual can make the decision to not share any data, to donate the data to charity, to allow others a one-time use of it, to sell their data on a subscription model, or to provide unlimited access to it.

One company, Humanity.co is pioneering this model of "consent as a service." As personal data is recognized as a human right, the ownership of that data is in the hands of each individual. Consent as a service helps every individual manage their personal data and protect their privacy. Brands realize that competing on asking users for consent for their personal data and on personal data privacy can become a market differentiator as well as an ethical approach. People who choose to be compensated for sharing data can be paid, while those who want to protect their privacy can easily exercise that option. For example, in the drug discovery process, global pharmaceutical companies pay between $400 and $800 for a patient record that is reconstructed from pharmacy records—data that is available for resale—depending on the potential benefits of the drug research. Imagine if a global pharmaceutical company could just pay the patient directly and offer them $800 to $1,000 per year for that data. As the founder and CEO, Richie Etwaru notes, this is a fight for the thirty-first human right—a reference to the United Nation's list of thirty international human rights. As more company leaders and policymakers understand the need to put personal data back in the hands of individuals as a way to prevent abuse by digital giants, expect support for the thirty-first human right to increase.[13]

3. ENCOURAGE ENTREPRENEURSHIP WITH START-UP FRIENDLY POLICIES

While anti-trust laws and other regulations can even the playing field for competing against digital giants, we should also improve the conditions that spark entrepreneurship via legislation.

For example, the April 5, 2012, signing of the U.S. JOBS Act (Jumpstart Our Business Startups Act), removed regulatory barriers to creating startups while improving the ability to raise funds. One provision of the act made it easier to raise money through crowdfunding by increasing the number of shareholders needed before a company is required to register its common stock with the SEC and become a publicly reporting company. Emerging growth companies were also redefined as being those with less than $1 billion in total annual gross revenues, and were no longer expected to complete certain regulatory and disclosure requirements in the registration statement they file before going public or for a period of five years after that. Among other provisions, the bill also lifted the ban on general solicitation and advertising of specific kinds of private placements of securities. The Regulation A limit for securities offerings were raised from $5 million to $50 million, enabling larger fundraising efforts. The result of this legislation was expanded opportunities for crowdfunding and raising funds for new ideas. It created a foundation for an entrepreneur-friendly IPO on-ramp and made it more attractive for investors to fund startups. In of the age of digital giants, a similar mechanism will be necessary to fund digital giants to battle incumbents through debt and equity crowdfunding.

With fewer players in each market, government has a role in improving the entrepreneurial ecosystem. From reducing regulations that inhibit entrepreneurship to helping to attract capital, governments can actively improve the competitive landscape in a world of digital giants. For example, given the current appetite for remote work and the easy availability of technology that can make that happen, governments could encourage more entrepreneurial opportunities outside of the density of current tech hubs like Silicon Valley, Seattle, Austin, Bangalore, Hanzhou, London, Paris, or New York. This would spread out tech talent around the country and encourage digital giants and competitors to invest in new regions, spreading the growth and expansion of the talent networks needed to guide startups through digital giant ecosystems geographically. Governments might encourage these entrepreneurial opportunities in locations that have a strong STEM higher education facility, a growing ecosystem of technology talent and startups, land prices that enable single income earners to purchase property, great critical infrastructure such as internet connectivity, areas open to redevelopment and offering limited-term tax relief, and access to cheap computing power.

Final Word

How we plan for the arrival of the age of digital giants must be balanced with proactive policies that encourage innovation and competition. We are in the first phase of the lifecycle of digital giants—and we'll be living with them for quite some time.

Investment in these three critical areas today will help rewrite the narrative of how digital giants compete, and whether they will ensure free market access, equal opportunity, a level playing field, and all the public benefits and social good that the age of digital giants has to offer.

NOTES

1. THE RISE OF DUOPOLIES

1. Noel Tichy and Ram Charan, "Speed, Simplicity, Self-Confidence: An Interview with Jack Welch," *Harvard Business Review*, September–October, 1989. Accessed at https://hbr.org/1989/09/speed-simplicity-self-confidence-an-interview-with-jack-welch.
2. Rick Clough, "GE's $500,000,000,000 Market Wipeout Is Like Erasing Facebook," Bloomberg, October 1, 2018. Accessed at https://www.bloomberg.com/news/articles/2018-10-01/ge-s-500-000-000-000-market-wipeout-is-like-erasing-facebook.
3. Clayton M. Christensen, *The Innovator's Dilemma* (Harvard Business School Press, 1997).

2. THRIVING IN A WORLD OF DIGITAL GIANTS

1. Jim Chappelow, "Prisoner's Dilemma," Investopedia, updated May 23, 2019. Accessed at https://www.investopedia.com/terms/p/prisoners-dilemma.asp.
2. "Antoine Augustin Cournot, 1801–1877," The New School, defunct site accessed through Internet Archive. Accessed at https://web.archive.org/web/20080509153657/http://cepa.newschool.edu/het/profiles/cournot.htm.
3. "Bertrand's Duopoly Model (With Diagram)," EconomicsDiscussion, n.d. Accessed at https://www.economicsdiscussion.net/oligopoly/bertrands-duopoly-model-with-diagram/5396.
4. "Chamberlin's Monopolistic Competition," Policonomics, n.d. Accessed at https://policonomics.com/chamberlins-monopolistic-competition/.
5. Apple versus Google market share in app stores taken from Constellation internal research/estimates.
6. Apple versus Google revenue in app stores taken from Constellation internal research/estimates.

7. "Apple's App Store Ecosystem Facilitated over Half a Trillion Dollars in Commerce in 2019," Apple newsroom, press release, June 15, 2020. Accessed at https://www.apple.com/newsroom/2020/06/apples-app-store -ecosystem-facilitated-over-half-a-trillion-dollars-in-commerce-in-2019/.

8. Mansoor Iqbal, "App Download and Usage Statistics (2020)," Business of Apps, October 15, 2020. Accessed at https://www.businessofapps.com /data/app-statistics/.

9. Stephen Warwick, "Apple Developers have Earned Over $155 Billion Since the App Store's Launch in 2008," iMore.com, March 13, 2020. Accessed at https://www.imore.com/developers-have-earned-over-155-billion -app-stores-launch-2008.

10. "Dr. Vinton Cerf and Dr. Robert Kahn, Medal of Freedom Recipients," The White House, President George W. Bush, n.d. Accessed at https:// georgewbush-whitehouse.archives.gov/government/cerf-kahn-bio.html.

11. "FTC Order Settles Charges that FMC Corp. and Japan's Asahi Chemical Co. Engaged in Illegal Anticompetitive Practices," Federal Trade Commission, December 21, 2000. Accessed at https://www.ftc.gov /news-events/press-releases/2000/12/ftc-order-settles-charges-fmc-corp- and-japans-asahi-chemical-co.

12. "General Electric Company, In the Matter of," Federal Trade Commission, updated January 30, 2004. Accessed at https://www.ftc.gov/enforcement /cases-proceedings/0310097/general-electric-company-matter.

13. "FTC Orders Significant Divestitures in Clearing Valeros Acquisition of Kaneb Services and Pipe Line Partners," Federal Trade Commission, June 15, 2005. Accessed at https://www.ftc.gov/news-events/press -releases/2005/06/ftc-orders-significant-divestitures-clearing-valeros -acquisition.

14. "FTC Challenges Proposed Merger of Sysco and US Foods," Federal Trade Commission, February 19, 2015. Accessed at https://www.ftc.gov /news-events/press-releases/2015/02/ftc-challenges-proposed-merger -sysco-us-foods.

15. Thomas Sullivan, "Mallinckrodt to Pay $100M to Settle Antitrust Violations," Policy & Medicine, May 5, 2018. Accessed at https://www.policymed .com/2017/01/mallinckrodt-to-pay-100m-to-settle-antitrust-violations.html.

16. Treaty on European Union and Treaty on the Functioning of the European Union: Consolidated Versions as published at Official Journal of the European Union in 7 June 2016 (International Law Book 1).

3. BUSINESS UNUSUAL: THE AGE OF DUOPOLIES

1. Michael B. Sauter, Evan Comen, Thomas C. Frohlich and Samuel Stebbins, "Cheetos Lip Balm, Google+ and New Coke Among the 50 Worst Product Flops of All Time," USA Today, April 25, 2019 (updated May 27, 2019). Accessed at https://www.usatoday.com/story/money/2019/04

/25/50-worst-product-flops-of-all-time-include-new-coke-cheetos
-lip-balm/39380281/.

2. Michael B. Sauter, Evan Comen, Thomas C. Frohlich and Samuel Stebbins, "Cheetos Lip Balm, Google+ and New Coke Among the 50 Worst Product Flops of All Time."

3. "A Brief History of Salesforce.com, 1999–2020" salesforce.com website, March 13, 2020. Accessed at https://www.salesforceben.com/brief-history -salesforce-com/.

4. John R. Graham, Campbell R. Harvey, and Shivaram Rajgopal, "The Economic Implications of Corporate Financial Reporting," SSRN, January 11, 2005. Accessed at http://dx.doi.org/10.2139/ssrn.491627.

5. Brandon Kochkodin, "U.S. Airlines Spent 96% of Free Cash Flow on Buybacks," Bloomberg, March 16, 2020. Accessed at https://www.bloomberg .com/news/articles/2020-03-16/u-s-airlines-spent-96-of-free-cash-flow -on-buybacks-chart.

6. Al Ramadan, Dave Peterson, Christopher Lochhead, and Kevin Maney, *Play Bigger: How Pirates, Dreamers, and Innovators Create and Dominate Markets* (New York: HarperCollins, 2016).

7. R "Ray" Wang, "Constellation Research's 2020 Digital Transformation Survey," May 2020.

8. "The Tax Policy Center's Briefing Book," Tax Policy Center, updated May 2020. Accessed at https://www.taxpolicycenter.org/briefing-book /what-tcja-repatriation-tax-and-how-does-it-work.

9. Multiple articles in *The Economic Times* (English edition). Accessed on October 22, 2020 at https://economictimes.indiatimes.com/topic/Reliance -Jio-investment.

4. INSIDE THE BUSINESS AND MONETIZATION MODELS THAT POWER DATA GIANTS

1. Alison Griswold, "A Dot-com Era Deal with Amazon Marked the Beginning of the End for Toys R Us," Quartz, September 18, 2017. Accessed at https://qz.com/1080389/a-dot-com-era-deal-with-amazon-marked-the -beginning-of-the-end-for-toys-r-us/.

2. "What Went Wrong: The Demise of Toys R Us," Knowledge @ Wharton, University of Pennsylvania, March 4, 2018. Accessed at https:// knowledge.wharton.upenn.edu/article/the-demise-of-toys-r-us/.

3. Alison Griswold, "A Dot-com Era Deal with Amazon Marked the Beginning of the End for Toys R Us."

4. Alison Griswold, "A Dot-com Era Deal with Amazon Marked the Beginning of the End for Toys R Us."

5. "Adobe Acquires EchoSign," Adobe News, July 17, 2011. Accessed at https://news.adobe.com/news/news-details/2011/Adobe-Acquires -EchoSign/default.aspx.

6. "Adobe Buys e-Signature Company EchoSign," *Los Angeles Times*, July 18, 2011. Accessed at https://latimesblogs.latimes.com/technology/2011/07 /adobe-buys-e-signature-company-echosign.html.

7. "Adobe Fast Facts," Adobe website. Accessed at https://www.adobe .com/about-adobe/fast-facts.html.

8. Virginia Backaitis, "Adobe's Magento Buy Could Disrupt Digital Commerce And Digital Marketing Software Makers," Seeking Alpha, May 31, 2018. Accessed at https://seekingalpha.com/article/4178469-adobes-magento -buy-disrupt-digital-commerce-and-digital-marketing-software-makers.

9. "Adobe Acquires Allegorithmic, the Leader in 3D Editing and Authoring for Gaming and Entertainment," Adobe press release, January 23, 2019. Accessed at https://www.adobe.com/content/dam/acom/en/investor -relations/pdfs/01232019AdobeAcquiresAllegorithmic_Final.pdf.

10. "Adobe Completes Acquisition of Marketo," Adobe press release, October 31, 2018. Accessed at https://www.adobe.com/content/dam/acom/en /investor-relations/pdfs/103118AdobeCompletesAcquisitionMarketo.pdf.

11. "Adobe Completes Acquisition of Magento Commerce," Adobe press release, June 19, 2018. Accessed at https://news.adobe.com/news/news -details/2018/Adobe-Completes-Acquisition-of-Magento-Commerce /default.aspx.

12. "Adobe to Acquire TubeMogul," Adobe press release, November 10, 2016. Accessed at https://www.adobe.com/content/dam/acom/en/investor -relations/pdfs/AdobeToAcquireTubeMogul.pdf.

13. "Adobe to Acquire Fotolia: Adds Stock Content Marketplace to Creative Cloud," Adobe press release, December 11, 2014. Accessed at https:// www.adobe.com/content/dam/acom/en/investor-relations/pdfs /AdobetoAcquireFotolia.pdf.

14. "Adobe to Acquire Neolane, Extending Leadership in Digital Marketing," Adobe press release, June 27, 2013. Accessed at https://www.adobe .com/content/dam/acom/en/investor-relations/pdfs/062713Adobeto AcquireNeolane.pdf.

15. "Adobe Completes Acquisition of Efficient Frontier," Adobe press release, January 16, 2012. Accessed at https://www.adobe.com/content/dam /acom/en/investor-relations/pdfs/011612AdobeCloseEfficientFrontier.pdf.

16. Erick Schonfeld, "Adobe Buys Swiss Company Day Software for $240 Million," TechCrunch, July 28, 2010. Accessed at https://techcrunch .com/2010/07/27/adobe-buys-day-software-240-million/.

17. Don Clark and Suzanne Vranica, "Adobe to Acquire Omniture in $1.8 Billion Deal," *The Wall Street Journal*, September 16, 2009. Accessed at https://www.wsj.com/articles/SB125304615573813275.

18. Manik Ghawri, "Audiobooks Are Officially the Trendsetters in Publishing Industry," Businessworld, October 26, 2019. Accessed at http://www .businessworld.in/article/Audiobooks-Are-Officially-The-Trendsetters -In-Publishing-Industry-/26-10-2019-177957/.

19. Tien Tzuo and Gabe Weisert, *Subscribed: Why the Subscription Model Will Be Your Company's Future—and What to Do About It* (Portfolio, 2018).

20. Airline data 2010–2019 compiled by Constellation Research, Inc.

21. "Background," Star Alliance website, updated October 18, 2019. Accessed at https://www.staralliance.com/en/background.

22. Skyteam webpage. Accessed at https://www.skyteam.com/en.

23. Oneworld members webpage. Accessed at https://www.oneworld.com/members.

24. "Aeroplan," Wikipedia article. Accessed at https://en.wikipedia.org/wiki/Aeroplan

25. Aeroplan eStore webpage. Accessed at https://www.aeroplan.com/estore/.

26. "A Timeline of Aeroplan's History," Toronto City News, August 3, 2018. Accessed at https://toronto.citynews.ca/2018/08/03/a-timeline-of-aeroplans-history/.

27. Singapore Air press release. Accessed at https://www.singaporeair.com/en_UK/es/media-centre/press-release/article/?q=en_UK/2018/January-March/ne0518-180205.

28. James Henderson, "How Singapore Airlines Is Building Customer Loyalty Through Blockchain," *CIO*, July 18, 2019. Accessed at https://www.cio.com/article/3410316/how-singapore-airlines-is-building-customer-loyalty-through-blockchain.html.

29. Sheila Shayon, "6 Reasons for Singapore Airlines' Blockchain-Based Loyalty Program," Brandchannel, February 15, 2018. Accessed at https://www.brandchannel.com/2018/02/15/singapore-airlines-blockchain/.

5. PURSUE DECISION VELOCITY

1. Cited in *Military Air Power: The Cadre Digest of Air Power Opinions and Thoughts*, compiled by Lt. Col. Charles M. Westenhoff (Air University Press, October 1990).

2. LinkedIn webpage. Accessed at https://about.linkedin.com/.

3. "Philips Strengthens Collaboration with Amazon Web Services to Expand Digital Health Solutions in the Cloud," Philips news center, press release, October 9, 2015. Accessed at https://www.usa.philips.com/a-w/about/news/archive/standard/news/press/2015/20151008-Philips-strengthens-collaboration-Amazon-Web-Services-expand-digital-health-solutions-in-cloud.html.

4. "Samsung Will Replace Current Note7 with New One," Samsung newsroom press release, September 2, 2016. Accessed at https://news.samsung.com/global/statement-on-galaxy-note7.

5. Que Dallara, "How Industrial IoT Will Solve the Problems of the Next 20 Years," Honeywell Forge, n.d. Accessed at https://www.honeywell.com/en-us/honeywell-forge/problems-of-the-next-20-years.

6. DESIGN FOR A LONG-TERM MINDSET

1. James Clear, "40 Years of Stanford Research Found That People with This One Quality Are More Likely to Succeed," Jamesclear.com, n.d. Accessed at https://jamesclear.com/delayed-gratification.

2. Michale Birshan, Thomas Meanin, and Kurt Strovink, "Short-Term Pain for Long-Term Gain: The New CEO's Dilemma," McKinsey & Company, April 22, 2019. Accessed at https://www.mckinsey.com/business-functions/strategy-and-corporate-finance/our-insights/short-term-pain-for-long-term-gain-the-new-ceos-dilemma.

3. Adi Ignatius, "The Truth About CEO Tenure," *Harvard Business Review*, November–December, 2019. Accessed at https://hbr.org/2019/11/the-truth-about-ceo-tenure.

4. "CEO Tenure Drops to Just Five Years," Equilar, January 19, 2018. Accessed at https://www.equilar.com/blogs/351-ceo-tenure-drops-to-five-years.html.

5. "CEO Turnover Report," Challenger, Gray & Christmas, Inc., 2020. Accessed at http://www.challengergray.com/tags/ceo-turnover-report.

6. Peter Thiel, "Competition Is for Losers," *The Wall Street Journal,* September 12, 2014. Accessed at https://www.wsj.com/articles/peter-thiel-competition-is-for-losers-1410535536.

7. Information drawn from a 2020 Constellation Research Study on the Rule of 40.

8. Kim S. Nash, "Amazon, Alphabet and Walmart Were Top IT Spenders in 2018," *The Wall Street Journal*, January 17, 2019. Accessed at https://www.wsj.com/articles/amazon-alphabet-and-walmart-were-top-it-spenders-in-2018-11547754757.

9. Chris Cumming, "Private Equity's Trillion-Dollar Piggy Bank Holds Little for Struggling Companies," *The Wall Street Journal*, June 28, 2020. Accessed at https://www.wsj.com/articles/private-equitys-trillion-dollar-piggy-bank-holds-little-for-struggling-companies-11593212136.

10. "How Large Is the Leveraged Loan Market?" Bank of England, January 25, 2019. Accessed at https://www.bankofengland.co.uk/bank-overground/2019/how-large-is-the-leveraged-loan-market.

11. Navadha Pandey and Devansh Sharma, "3 Years After Launch, Jio Becomes No. 1 Telco by User Base, Revenue," Mint, January 17, 2020. Accessed at https://www.livemint.com/industry/telecom/reliance-jio-is-the-largest-telco-in-india-trai-11579180602386.html.

12. "Jio Investor Relations," Reliance, updated September 2020. Accessed at https://www.ril.com/OurBusinesses/Jio/Jio-Investor-Relations.aspx.

7. PARTNER OR BE PUNISHED

1. Paul Greenberg, *The Commonwealth of Self-Interest: Business Success Through Customer Engagement* (56 Group, LLC, 2019).
2. "IBM Food Trust: A New Era for the World's Food Supply," IBM blockchain webpage. Accessed at https://www.ibm.com/blockchain/solutions/food-trust.
3. "IBM Food Trust: A New Era for the World's Food Supply."

8. WHERE DO WE GO FROM HERE?

1. "Save the World and Benefit Mankind," BeiDou Navigation Satellite System webpage. Accessed at http://en.beidou.gov.cn.
2. Matthew Fox, "5 Companies Now Make Up 20% of the S&P 500. Here's Why Goldman Sachs Says That's a Bad Signal for Future Market Returns. (MSFT, AAPL, AMZN, GOOGL, FB)," *Business Insider*, April 7, 2020. Accessed at https://markets.businessinsider.com/news/stocks/sp500-concentration-large-cap-bad-sign-future-returns-effect-market-2020-4-1029133505.
3. Danny Palmer, "What Is the Tesla Semi? Everything You Need to Know About Tesla's Semi-Autonomous Electric Truck," Zdnet, March 22, 2018. Accessed at https://www.zdnet.com/article/what-is-the-tesla-semi-everything-you-need-to-know-about-teslas-semi-autonomous-electric-truck/.
4. "Real Money Will Be in Services for Apple: Tech Watcher," Fox Business video, December 17, 2019. Accessed at https://video.foxbusiness.com/v/6116464870001/#sp=show-clips.
5. Leena Rao, "Apple Pay Volume Up 500% in Latest Quarter," *Fortune*, October 25, 2016. Accessed at https://fortune.com/2016/10/25/apple-pay-volume/.
6. Lan Liang, Ph.D., Brian Moore, Ph.D., and Anita Soni, Ph.D., "National Inpatient Hospital Costs: The Most Expensive Conditions by Payer, 2017," Agency for Healthcare Research and Quality, Healthcare Cost and Utilization Project, July 2020. Accessed at https://www.hcup-us.ahrq.gov/reports/statbriefs/sb261-Most-Expensive-Hospital-Conditions-2017.jsp.
7. Research & Care webpage. Accessed at https://www.researchandcare.org.
8. Haven webpage, vision statement. Accessed at https://havenhealthcare.com/vision.
9. Pill Pack by Amazon Pharmacy, press page. Accessed at https://www.pillpack.com/press.
10. "Fitbit to Be Acquired by Google," Fitbit press release, November 1, 2019. Accessed at https://investor.fitbit.com/press/press-releases/press-release-details/2019/Fitbit-to-Be-Acquired-by-Google/default.aspx.
11. Clayton Christensen, *The Innovator's Dilemma*.

12. "Critical Infrastructure Sectors," Cybersecurity & Infrastructure Security Agency, n.d. Accessed at https://www.cisa.gov/critical-infrastructure -sectors.
13. Tyler Wetzel, "Complete Ownership Over Your Data Is the New 31st Human Right," Medium, November 7, 2018. Accessed at https:// medium.com/predict/complete-ownership-over-your-data-is-the -new-31st-human-right-2c16d1b4bd93.

INDEX

Over the past twenty-five years I've been an analyst and trusted advisor for more than a thousand global organizations and leading brands, giving me a front row seat to the changes that have led us to the extraordinary rise of ducat polies. Throughout the book, I cited research from my firm, Constellation Research. Unless otherwise cited, Constellation, Research was the source for the data cited. Constellation Research's work can be found at www.constellationr.com.